PVT. JOHN C. WEST

A TEXAN
IN SEARCH OF
A FIGHT

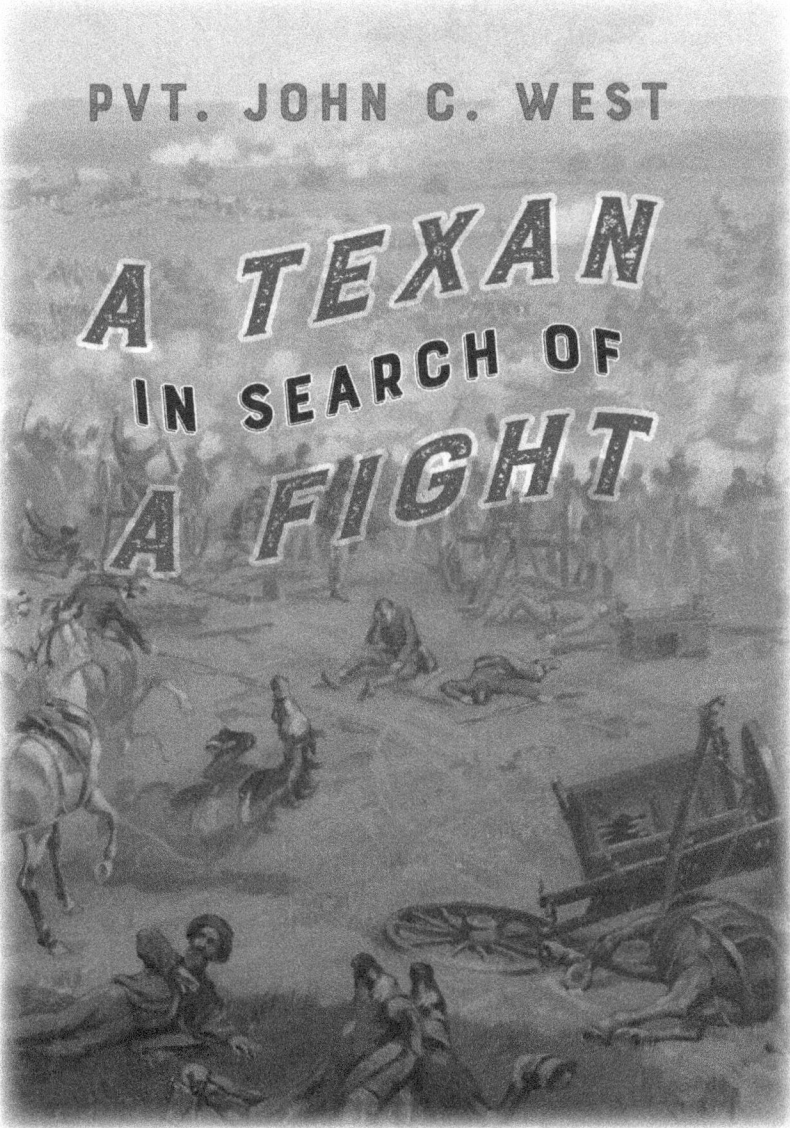

Copano Bay Press
2019

Originally published in 1903 under the same title, privately by the author.

Design copyright Copano Bay Press 2019
ISBN 978-1-941324-73-8

TO THE WOMEN OF THE SOUTH THIS BOOK IS RESPECTFULLY DEDICATED.

By their smiles they inspired and encouraged the soldiers in the field. By their frowns and scorn they drove the laggards to the front. By their tears, their sympathy and their prayers they upheld and stimulated the weak, the weary and the wounded.

Their unfailing faith, their sublime devotion to truth were not surpassed by the glorious heroism of the noble women whose names sanctify and adorn the history of ages past. Their sacrifices, their toils, their fidelity, their sufferings entitle them to the love, admiration and gratitude of posterity, which ought to be demonstrated by the erection of a shining shaft of marble—white, pure and chaste—whose apex shall kiss the clouds.

PREFACE

The following pages were put in type-written form in 1897. Until that time I had not seen the originals for thirty-four years. The manuscript has been read by persons of ability, learning and intelligence. Many of them said it was valuable and ought to be published. I had never thought of this. It was intended only for convenient use among my family and immediate friends. Requests and suggestions for its publication have recently been renewed. With hesitation I have consented. The questions of taste, delicacy and propriety of publishing private matter have been considered and discussed. The conclusion is that it should be printed and issued, word for word, as it was originally written thirty-eight years ago. Otherwise it would not be what the writer wrote and thought in those dark, historic days. It is not fiction. It is fact. Under the head of "Addenda," I have added "The Story of a Blanket," by request. Also a speech made at McGregor in 1897. The diary and the speech illustrate, respectively, the Confederate soldier of 1863 and the reconstructed citizen of 1897.   —J. C. W.

EXPLANATORY STATEMENT

In order that the following pages may be better under-stood, it is proper to make a short statement of facts as to the writer, and especially is this statement necessary to explain the frequent references to Camden and to Co-lumbia, South Carolina, because, while I have now been in Texas since 1855, and have been identified with and loved her history for forty-five years, yet at the time this diary of "A TEXAN IN SEARCH OF A FIGHT" was written, I had only been absent from South Carolina about six years, and all the associations of my boyhood and youth were fresh and green and my young heart was hardly weaned from its attachment to the precious memories of college days.

I was born in Camden, South Carolina, April 12, 1834; was prepared for college by Leslie McCandless, Esq.; entered college December, 1851, sophomore class; was honorably dismissed with over one hundred others De-cember, 1852, on account of the so-called "biscuit re-bellion;" returned and re-entered junior class in June, 1858; graduated December, 1854; came to Texas De-cember, 1855; returned to Columbia, South Carolina, and married Miss Mary E. Stark, April 14, 1858; enlisted in the first company raised for Confederate service in McLennan county in 1861—Captain Ryan.

I was the only married man in the company, and on this account was entreated very earnestly by the oldest and best citizens not to enlist, but I thought it was my duty to go and was anxious to go. My wife, with two little children, was fifteen hundred miles from her kindred in South Carolina, but she agreed with me that every man ought to go. The matter was settled in a manner altogether unexpected by me. Before this company—afterwards Company E, Fourth Texas Regiment, Hood's Brigade—left the state, I was, on the 22d day of May, 1861, appointed by Hon. Jefferson Davis, district attorney of the Confederate States for the Western district of Texas, and entered upon the discharge of the duties of that office. This appointment was under the provisional government. After serving a few months, until about the 1st day of March, 1862, I determined to enter the military service. I enlisted in Speight's regiment and was afterwards transferred to Cook's heavy artillery, hoping and believing that there would be a fight at Galveston very soon.

On the 22d of April, 1862, I was again appointed district attorney for the Western district of Texas under permanent government, but remained with my company until July 2, 1862, when I was discharged and again entered upon the peaceful pursuits of prosecuting criminals against the laws of the Confederacy, which I pursued diligently until April 9, 1863, at which time, being more determined than ever to see a fight, and to remain in the ranks, if necessary, until the close of the war, I enlisted in my original old company, which had long since become Company E, Fourth Texas Regiment. Lieutenant Thomas J. Selman had come to Texas for recruits. I enlisted with him on April 9 and started from Waco, Texas, for the Virginia army on April 11, 1863, which is the first date in the diary which follows this statement, and in verification of it I here add a copy of my commission as district attorney, also of the law of the Confederacy under which I left the office for the army, also my certificate of discharge from the army at Galveston, Texas.

AN ACT FOR THE RELIEF OF DISTRICT ATTORNEYS
OF THE CONFEDERATE STATES IN THE FIELD.
The Congress of the Confederate States of America do enact:
That wherever a district attorney of the Confederate States
may enter the military service of the Confederate States he
may by the consent of the district judge, entered of record,
appoint an attorney pro tempore during his absence. Approved
May 21, 1861.

Under this law I appointed Hon. N. O. Green, of San
Antonio, Texas, as district attorney pro tempore, with
the consent of Hon. Thos. J. Devine, then Confederate
States District Judge for the Western District of Texas.

The following is a copy of my commission under the
permanent government of the Confederate States, the
original of which is now in my possession:

Jefferson Davis, President of the Confederate States of America:

To all who shall see these presents, greeting: Know ye that re-
posing special trust and confidence in the integrity, ability and
punctuality of John C. West, I have nominated, and by and with
the advice and consent of the senate do appoint him attorney
for the Western District of Texas, and do authorize and empow-
er him to execute and fulfill the duties of that office according
to law and to have and to hold the said office with all the powers, privileges and emoluments to the same of right appertain-
ing unto him, the said John C. West, subject to the provisions of
the Constitution and the Laws of the Confederate States.

In testimony whereof I have caused these letters to be made
patent and the seal of the Confederate States to be hereunto
affixed.

Given under my hand, at the City of Richmond the twenty-sec-
ond day of April, in the year of our Lord, one thousand eight
hundred and sixty-two.   By the President:

JEFFERSON DAVIS

(SEAL)
J. P. BENJAMIN
Secretary of State

SOLDIER'S DISCHARGE

To all Whom it May Concern:

Know ye, That John C. West, private of Captain D. G. Adams' Company, First Regiment of Artillery, who was enlisted the first day of March, one thousand eight hundred and sixty-two, to serve one year, is hereby honorably discharged from the Army of the Confederate States, by reason of his appointment as district attorney for the Western District of Texas, under a commission issued by the President. Said John C. West was born in Camden, in the State of South Carolina, is twenty-eight years of age, five feet seven inches high, fair complexion, blue eyes, light hair, and by occupation when enlisted an attorney at law.

Given at Galveston, this the seventh day of July, 1862.

> D. G. ADAMS,
> Captain, Commanding Company K

Approved:
JOHN H. MANLY
Lt. Col. Commanding Regiment

The following pages are copied from a diary kept from April 9, 1863, to June 9, 1863, as I find it written in lead pencil in a small notebook carried for that purpose. I have not read it since 1863, and find that it is fading and becoming indistinct. On the outside cover of this book are these words:

JOHN C. WEST

CONFEDERATE STATES DISTRICT ATTORNEY,
WESTERN DISTRICT OF TEXAS.

WACO, JUNE, 1862

PRIVATE, COMPANY E,
FOURTH TEXAS REGIMENT,
ROBERTSON'S BRIGADE,
HOOD'S DIVISION

APRIL 9, 1863

This careless little journal is useless to a stranger, but may be prized by my friends. If its owner cannot be found, let it be sent to Major Theodore Stark, Columbia, South Carolina.

JOHN CAMDEN WEST

THE DIARY

Left Waco, Texas, on the morning of April 11, 1863; bid adieu to my dear little Stark and Mary at home; said goodbye to my sweet wife at the ferryboat landing (at the foot of Bridge street). Nothing of interest occurred on the way to Springfield, (about forty miles east of Waco); saw two or three prairie chickens and a green sportsman trying to kill one; saw at Springfield, as I had left at Waco, a good many stout, able-bodied patriots, who, somehow, kept out of the service; stopped at Mc-Cracken's, fifteen miles east of Springfield, for the night; found Mr. McCracken a strong Houston man and would vote for him for governor if he "had to be hauled to the polls in a wagon."

I fear there are too many of this kind and others worse, who will elect Houston if he runs. His election will be an invitation to Yankee invasion. However honest he may be in his devotion to the South, the North would regard his election as an endorsement of his past action.

APRIL 12th.

Left McCracken's at 3 o'clock in the morning. It is my birthday. I am 29 years old today (Sunday). Reached Fairfield (70 miles east of Waco) at breakfast; found it quite a neat little town with a large female seminary, but did not stay long enough to walk about the place. Came on to Parker's Bluff, twenty-five miles, for dinner, having passed through a sandy, post-oak country until we reached the Trinity bottom, which is a magnificently fertile spot. The Trinity is a narrow stream with very steep banks, resembling a bayou. Mr. Ward was our host and fed us bountifully on venison and wild turkey. The woods were full of game. We remained at Parker's Bluff

11

until 2 o'clock p.m. on the 13th. There was a gentle norther on the 12th and pretty hard rain on the 13th.

My traveling companions were Lieutenant Selman, Coella Mullins and Burrell Aycock, all of the Fourth Texas regiment, bound for Richmond, Va.

APRIL 13th.

Left Parker's Bluff at 2 o'clock; roads very muddy and one balky horse to contend with. The driver insisted that he would do very well after he became heated. As the sun was very warm the horse accommodated us by getting heated very soon and gave us very little trouble. Within about four miles of Palestine one hind wheel of the coach gave way and we sank very gently into the road. After considerable delay we placed a sliding pole under the axle and went on our way rejoicing, on foot. We strolled into Palestine about 5 o'clock in the afternoon. It has an older and more settled look than the towns in western Texas. The court house square is shaded by very pretty sycamore trees. It is situated in a hilly, red clay region. About one-third of the buildings are brick and the balance are framed buildings. We discovered here some defect in our transportation tickets, and will have to pay our way to Rusk. It will be just my luck to have to pay all the way to Richmond, Va. I have already paid out since the war commenced five times as much for the privilege of serving in the ranks as the government has paid me, but I am perfectly willing to give all I have if the sacrifice will aid my country in achieving its liberty.

Tuesday, APRIL 14th.

Left Palestine about 5 o'clock a.m., in a two-horse wagon; same company, with the addition of Mr. Mathus of the First Texas. The ride to Rusk would have been insupportably dull but for good company; nothing but red clay hills and deep gullies, ornamented with pine and oak. It, however, brought up some pleasing reminiscences of old South Carolina and my boyhood days—the season when ambitious hopes burned in my breast and I determined I would be a man—little dreaming then that I would have the satisfaction of striking a blow in the holiest cause that ever tired the breast of man, and illustrating by action the feelings which glowed and burned in my little heart, on reading the stories of Wallace and of Tell.

We reached Rusk about 4 o'clock in the afternoon without an incident of interest, and found W. G. Thomas to be the quartermaster there. He appears to be an accommodating and clever officer and refunded our transportation which we had paid out at Palestine.

Today is the fifth anniversary of my wedding day, and I have thought often of my dear wife and little ones and wished I could be with them, but I am resolved not to remain quietly at home another moment while a foe is on our soil.

Wednesday, APRIL 15th.

I went to the supper table last night too sick to eat anything; left the table and laid down on a lounge until the hotel keeper could show me a room; I retired early and slept well; got up this morning all right, but did not go to the breakfast table; took a lunch from my own haversack; walked out in town; went to the ten-pin alley and spent an hour rolling; had not played a game before for eight years, and enjoyed it very much; smoked a cigar, a notable scarcity in these times, and returned to the hotel, where I wrote a letter to Judge Devine, and one to my dear wife; may heaven's choicest blessings rest upon her and my sweet children; went to the dinner table and found the landlady apologizing for some defect and two young females discussing the merits of the

13

Episcopal and Baptist faith; got through dinner somehow and walked down to the quartermaster's office; got the Vicksburg Whig; stretched myself out on the counter; read and took a nap; got up; went to the armory and would have enjoyed looking over the work very much but felt sick; it produces four Mississippi rifles per day at $30.00 apiece on contract with the state; I am now sitting at the foot of the hill below the armory.

Friday, APRIL 17th.

I left Rusk on the morning of the 16th on a six passenger coach; there were fourteen aboard; the driver was skillful and the road good; I was suffering intensely from dysentery and had a high fever from breakfast time until sundown; oh, the long, long weary miles pent up in that crowded coach; I slept half an hour at Henderson; at the next stand I bathed in the horse bucket and my fever left me; I chewed a piece of salt ham; it was now dark; I laid down on top of the stage coach and was very comfortable about half of the night, but suffered tortures during the latter part of the night; reached Marshall about 7 o'clock in the morning; sent for a physician and will remain here for a day or two, until I am able to travel; Lieutenant Selman had a cup of genuine coffee made for me which I enjoyed very much; Burwell Aycock is trying to get a soft boiled egg for me; I think I will be well in a day or two; this attack was brought on by a check of perspiration after becoming overheated in the walk of four miles to Palestine.

Saturday, APRIL 18th.

I spent a very uncomfortable night; a dull, steady pain all night; had taken twenty drops of laudanum; had no matches and did not wish to disturb my companions; I did not sleep more than an hour; my friends left this morning for Alexandria via Shreveport; I could have

14

gone with them if my physician, Dr. Johnson, had kept his promise and given me medicine yesterday evening that would have insured a night's rest, but he was detained in the country by an urgent case. General Chambers thinks Texas ought to give three hundred and twenty acres of land for every newborn boy; the doctor came in about 8 o'clock in the morning, left three pills for me to take at intervals of two hours and a powder to be taken at bed time; I am getting on very well and will leave here on Monday, I think; I have just discovered that my pocketbook is lost, containing about sixty dollars; I am satisfied that I lost it off the top of the stage between here and the twelve mile stand this side of Rusk; I have had advertisements struck off to this effect, headed, "Lost! Lost!! the Last Red!" and asked the stage driver to have them posted on the road every five or six miles; since my pocketbook is gone I feel bound to accept the kind invitation of Mrs. Brownnigg, formerly Octavia Calhoun, to take a room in her house; she has just sent me a nice breakfast, and I have sent her word that I will come down.

I am at Mrs. Brownnigg's in a comfortable room; do not feel as if I were in the way as there is plenty of house room; Mrs. Bacon, formerly Anna Haralson, is here; she arrived yesterday and started to Georgia with Mr. Bacon, but became disgusted with the trip; she and Mrs. Brownnigg both treat me as kindly as though I were a brother, and I know my precious wife would feel very well satisfied if I could receive such treatment every time I am away from her, but there is no attention that approaches the gentle and delicate touch of a wife's hand, and there is no wife whose tenderness and sympathy can equal that of my Mary; I must forego the pleasure of her gentle words and smiles for a season, until the kindness of Providence brings us together again; I am located as well

15

here as I could possibly be at home and may God and good angels guard my benefactors.

Sunday, APRIL 19th.

I rested well last night but had the most hideous dreams all night; Mrs. Brownnigg came in early this morning and asked me into her room; I went and found the fire very comfortable; the doctor came to see me and seems to think I am all right now, but must be careful about my diet; says some good brandy is exactly what I need to recruit on; so I missed it by leaving mine at home. Major Holman called to see me this morning; says he will see my transportation fixed all right; offers relief from the loss of my pocketbook; the doctor does likewise; Mrs. Brownnigg offers me money also. I ate nice toast and drank genuine coffee for breakfast; had chicken soup for dinner; spent most of the day in reading one of Bulwer's novels, entitled, "A Strange Story"; have read fifty or sixty pages, but am not much interested yet. My intention now is to leave here so as to remain at Alexandria the shortest time possible. I learn today that Mr. A, my hotel landlord, is tired of soldiers, especially sick ones, and grumbles terribly when one gets out of money at his hotel. If this is true, he is not a true man. I would rather be under obligations to the devil.

Little Bettie Brownnigg is quite a nice girl. Hallie Bacon, several years younger, is in a fair way to be spoiled. There is a young lady, Miss Nora Gregg, staying with Mrs. Brownnigg; she seems to be a clever good girl and is finishing my sock, which wife expected Miss Nannie Norton, of Richmond, Va., to knit for me; she has knit thirty pairs of socks in the last two months; she has a most magnificent suit of soft brown hair.

Monday, APRIL 20th.

I was asleep the greater part of last night, but cannot call it rest. Oh! those hideous dreams which haunted me. I went to a market on Bridge street in Waco, where human flesh, sound and putrid, was bought and sold. I bought and ate, and made my children eat, then dreamed again. Oh! such horrid, phantastic and awful visions as only opium can breed! Fearful crimes were calmly concocted, and the darkest mysteries were enjoyed with devilish glee! Everything which was unholy, everything fiendish, damnable and impure seemed ever present. But the night and the dream have past, and let them be past forever! I am not so well today as yesterday, but do not think I will need any more medicine.

Major Holman came to see me again this morning. Mr. Lewis, an old gentleman, formerly clerk of the Federal Court at Tyler, also came to see me. He is just from Huntsville, Alabama, and gave me suggestions as to the route across the Mississippi. I took a whisky toddy this morning. Miss Beloy came in and brought a very fat, pretty baby, her little sister. She is an amiable looking girl—reminds me of sister Mac (Mrs. DeSanssure) as she looked in the golden old days when we were young and before so many friends had dropped like flowers in the tomb, and when Mac had lightly "supped sorrow." When I have tears to shed let them fall for the dread affliction of my friends, for Oh! how bitterly, bitterly my dear sisters, Mrs. M. B. and Mac DeS. have suffered!

Mrs. Bacon's little girl seems very sick today. I have been in Mrs. B's room lying on a lounge nearly all the morning.

17

Tuesday, APRIL 21st.

I went up town this morning; feel like I am growing stronger, but am suffering with a very sore mouth. Think I shall start for Shreveport on Tuesday. Have heard nothing of my pocketbook; paid the printer five dollars for handbills and one dollar for twenty envelopes. Heard today of the death of Captain Brownnigg; announced it to Mrs. Brownnigg; the effect was as might have been expected; I thought at first that she would not revive at all; she seems more quiet now. Major Holman promised to let me have money to continue my trip. I am about to commence a letter to my wife.

Wednesday, APRIL 22nd.

Got up this morning feeling pretty well and concluded to leave tomorrow; went up town and mailed a letter to my wife; saw Dr. Johnson and got a certificate from him accounting for my delay, and a mixture of chalk and laudanum to take on the road; had a long talk with the doctor and Rev. Mr. Wilson about the Downs and Sparks, citizens of Waco; the doctor refused to charge me anything. I borrowed seventy-five dollars from Major Holman and gave him my note. Have been reading Bulwer's "Strange Story" a good deal today. Mrs. Weir came in this evening and talked very kindly to me; wants me to stay longer, but I must go; every man ought to go. Witnessed a cock fight in the streets a few minutes ago and rather enjoyed it; wonder how my chickens come on at home, and what my dear wife and dear little Stark and Mary are doing now. Mrs. Bacon has just brought me a pocketbook, and she and Mrs. Brownnigg and Mrs. Weir have offered me money. Miss Gregg has brought me a toddy and I must drink it. Oh! these women!

The world was sad, the garden was a wild,
And man, the hermit, sighed till woman smiled.

Thursday, APRIL 23rd.

Got up early this morning and read Bulwer's "Strange Story" until called to breakfast; after breakfast went to the cars and started to Shreveport; the track is laid for sixteen miles to Jonesville; we traveled over this at very good speed, jolting and swinging a good deal; at Jonesville we took a stage and dragged along for five miles very slowly, but after changing horses got on very well to Mrs. Eppe's, where we had the only nice meal I have found at any place on the road; reached Shreveport about 3:30 p.m.; stopped at the Veranda; went to the quartermaster and got transportation to Alexandria; went down to see the gunboat, *Missouri*, now being built. I do not understand technicalities well enough to describe her; she is about 120 feet long and the most solid, massive piece of work I ever saw, covered with railroad iron. I started out with Lieutenant Ochiltree to find a private boarding house; found one; don't know the name of the proprietress; charges two dollars per day; sent our baggage around; took a seat in front of quartermaster's office to look at the ladies passing, and other interesting sights; saw some really pretty ones and felt better for it; started home to supper and stopped to take a drink, saw a fight between a red-headed member of the Fourth Texas, from Navarro county, and a citizen of Shreveport; Fourth Texas was worsted and was carried off to the guard house; I went on to supper; after supper discovered a Baptist church on opposite side of the street lighted up; went over and found the minister and two men and four women holding prayer meeting; staid until the meeting closed and concluded that the Shreveport church was in a lukewarm condition; after church I stood in the street and heard a hopeful widow sing some very pretty songs; went back to my boarding house.

Friday, APRIL 24th.

Forgot to say in my diary yesterday that I met Mrs. Conrow, of Waco, and her son, Frank Harris, on their way to Arkadelphia; got up this morning and after breakfast walked up town; loafed about until 10 o'clock; engaged passage in the stage to Alexandria; went to boarding house and wrote a letter to my precious wife and one to my sister, Mrs. Mary West Blair, at Austin; came to town again, and have been witnessing a few games of billiards between Lieutenant Ochiltree and Devoussy, the daguerrean. I am bored to death and want to get away. Lieutenant Ochiltree let me have $35.00, which I am to pay over to Major T. S. Bass, of the First Texas, when I get to Richmond; I am not speaking of Tom Ochiltree, but Lieutenant W. B. Ochiltree, Adjutant Culberson's Eighteenth Regiment, Walker's Division.

Saturday, APRIL 25th.

Left Shreveport at 4 o'clock a.m. in a hack; had a fine pair of horses, and the day being cloudy, had quite a pleasant ride; got a good breakfast at Mr. Allen's; reached the Widow Gamble's about 1 o'clock. This is the most beautiful place I have seen since I left home; every tree has either a rose or a honeysuckle clambering over it, all fragrant and blooming; there is a Cherokee rose hedge all round the farm. This place is within six miles of poor Burney Means' home; he has gone to his rest, and my thoughts were all day of him and our dear old college days. We were fellow students in the South Carolina college; he was my closest and most confidential friend and his smiling face is photographed on my heart forever; I cannot yet fully realize that I shall never see him again.

Reached Mansfield about dark; a neat little village full of pretty girls.

Sunday, APRIL 26th.

Left Mansfield last night at 10 o'clock, and after a miserable, jolting ride of twenty-nine miles, got to the breakfast stand about 9 o'clock a.m. The road was better and the ride more agreeable for the next twenty-five or thirty miles, which brought me to Natchitoches, La. Met some militia-men, a few soldiers from Sibley's command, all of whom gave the most doleful account of affairs below, on Red river; said that General Kirby' Smith and all his staff and everything of military character had left Alexandria on a steamboat for Shreveport; that the Federals were within fourteen miles of Alexandria yesterday morning; that there were 50,000 of them. I do not believe more than half the rumors that are afloat, and am patiently awaiting the arrival of the stage, which left Alexandria last night, to learn something positive.

Monday, APRIL 27th.

After the stage arrived on yesterday evening, I learned that it had come from only about fifty miles below and is not going to Alexandria any more, but is only going forty miles in that direction in order to bring up the stock, etc., on the line. The rumor is that the Federals are in possession of Alexandria; all the troops are retreating in this direction.

I have spent a very disagreeable day; it has been raining all day and kept me confined to the house; I am in a quandary; don't know what to do or where to go; am staying at a Frenchman's house at two dollars and a half per day; have no friend or acquaintance to consult and am utterly at a loss whether to go back to Shreveport or to make an effort to go forward; am afraid to try the latter plan for fear of getting out of money too far from home; think I shall start back tomorrow night.

Read Lycidas' "L'Allegro" and "Il Penseroso" today, and a few chapters in "Old Mortality;" one of the longest and most disagreeable days I ever spent in my life; O, for peace and a quiet day with my dear wife and little darlings.

Tuesday, APRIL 28th.

Have spent another long and weary day and suffered all that is incident to a position of suspense and uncertainty; cannot tell what may await me yet, but thus far in the last three days have spent the most disagreeable period of my life. Read "Old Mortality" awhile this morning; walked up town; saw a good many drunken officers and a great deal of drinking; saw a game of billiards on a table without pockets; sixty points instead of one hundred make a game; came to my boarding house and read "Old Mortality" and tried to take a nap, but was too nervous to sleep. The stage from Mansfield has just arrived; I trust it will take a regular trip back and start early; anything to get out of this dead, still state of uncertainty; I would rather go into battle tomorrow than to remain in this position; it gives me too much time to think of home; there is no happiness in this. My French landlady mended my suspenders and made me a cup of coffee this afternoon; she seems to be a kind-hearted creature. We have just had a shower of rain and there is a most beautiful rainbow in the east.

Wednesday, APRIL 29th.

Left Natchitoches at 9 o'clock p.m. on Tuesday and had a very disagreeable ride, taking all night to get to Dutchman Cumberlando to breakfast; ate a strip of bacon and a piece of corn bread for which he charged me a dollar, and that on the heels of an invective against extortions and speculators. I saw on the road today large numbers of negroes from the lower parishes of Louisiana whose masters were retreating from the Yankee vandals; saw the tracks of several severe whirlwinds, which have occurred in the last three weeks; was quite sick for a while this afternoon and was not improved by hearing that all stragglers and recruits belonging across the Mississippi were to be detained on this side of Red river; reached Mansfield about 4:30 this afternoon; saw two young ladies riding on horseback; they worked very hard and their arms seemed to be in their way, dangled about very ungracefully; they, however, appeared to enjoy the ride very much.

Thursday APRIL 30th.

Left Mansfield at 4 o'clock this morning; had a delightful ride partly through groves of magnolia and beech to the breakfast stand, Mrs. Gamble's. This is the same beautiful place of which I have spoken before; roses and honeysuckles clinging on oaks and hickory. One beautiful cluster of roses was high up among the branches of an old oak which had lately died, its withered leaves still clinging to their places. I thought of fair young maidens bedecking with wreathes the tomb of some powerful giant. Oh, for peace and such a home as this with my precious wife and little darlings, with $10,000.00 per annum and an unwavering faith in the Bible; this would be paradise enough for me. I got an elegant breakfast here and talked a good deal with a sprightly widow who could not understand how one Confederate dollar could redeem another and make the currency any better; came to Mr. Allen's to dinner and had diverse and sundry vegetables; the first I have had this season; enjoyed them hugely. Reached Shreveport at 5 o'clock; washed and put on some clean clothes; the first in three weeks; got shaved and passed for a gentleman; went to the quartermaster's office and protested against my transportation being paid to Alexandria as the stage company failed to carry me there; met Colonel Bagley, of Sibley's brigade. He was wounded in the Bisland fight; told me that Captain Brownnigg was killed by the bursting of a shell, which killed his horse also. Lieutenant Ochiltree is to introduce me after supper to Captain Rice, of Houston, of the First Texas regiment. I am to consult with him about getting across the river; trust I may not be delayed any longer. Must find a fight on this side if I cannot get across the river. While I am writing this, my landlady, Mrs. ___, is thundering in my ears against the Baptists of Shreveport. She says they countenance thieving, false-swearing, etc. It is now 10 o'clock p.m. I have been up town; met Captain Wash Hill and Captain Dave Rice. Hill is just from Richmond and says it is impossible for me to get across the river. I will start, however, with Captain Rice tomorrow morning, for Monroe, and see what can be done. Attended a Baptist prayer meeting tonight; not spiritual enough; too cold.

Friday, MAY 1st.

After breakfast read the Marshall Republican; found a very good speech from Horatio Seymour, Democratic candidate for governor of New York.

Walked about town until I met Captain Rice. Engaged my seat on the stage for Monroe, Louisiana; found Bulwer's "Strange Story" in Captain Rice's room and read about twenty pages; spent the morning with Captain Rice and with Lieutenants Davis and Eastman; took dinner at the restaurant; went back home; wrote letters to my dear wife and to Mr. Carter; walked to the post office, and met Lieutenant Moore; went to the Veranda and took supper with him; met Hall of El Paso, Myers of Corpus Christi and Patrick of Leon county, Texas; spent the evening discussing our prospects of getting across the river.

Saturday, MAY 2nd.

Was told by S. N. Brogdon, on the stage, that, my old college classmate, Loudon Butler, was Captain of Company B, Nineteenth Louisiana regiment. Left Shreveport this morning at daylight and came through a very rich and pretty country for twenty-five or thirty miles; nearly all planted in corn; passed Mrs. Butler's plantation and heard of Loudon; he is in Mobile. Came to Minden by dark and inquired for Mr. Bayliss, formerly pastor of the First Baptist church at Waco, Texas, and learned that he had left a day or two before for the army; came on after dark to stage stand ten miles east of Minden. There I met gentlemen just from Natchez, who told me that my former companions, Lieutenant Selman, Burwell Aycock and Coella Mullens were on the other side of the river.

Monday, MAY 4th.

Traveled all night Saturday night, having left Minden at dark, and all day Sunday; reached Vianna about 10 o'clock Sunday morning; the road was pretty rough, lying mainly through a hilly country, covered with large pines and red and white oak; reached the dinner stand about 4 o'clock and found it a very neat and comfortable place; was waited upon at the table by two young ladies. Had a tedious and disagreeable ride from this place to Monroe, which place we reached at 12 o'clock last night; took possession of the flatboat and rowed ourselves across the river; found the hotel crowded and could not get a room; spread down my blanket and slept on the piazza; got up this morning and wrote a letter to my dear wife before breakfast; after breakfast walked down to see the *Anna*, the boat we expected to go down the river in; found her a dirty little craft; went to the quartermaster's office to find out when the boat would leave; he could not tell for two or three hours yet; returned to the hotel;

met Ormsby; he is in the post office department; he has a thousand pounds of postage stamps and is on his way to Texas.

I saw a very interesting game of poker between Captain R____ and a professional gambler; it was twenty dollars ante, and the pile grew fast and soon reached twenty-five hundred dollars, and everybody went out of the game except Captain R___ and the professional, who was a very rough looking customer, reminding me of descriptions I have read of pirates in yellow covered novels; he was weather-beaten and fierce looking; Capt. R___ was only about twenty years of age, with a beardless face as smooth as a woman's. A dispute arose and each man seized the pile (paper money) with his left hand and drew his pistol with his right; they rose at arm's length and stood glaring at each other like tigers; one looked like a black wolf, the other like a spotted leopard; the crowd retired from the table; it was one of the most fearful and magnificent pictures I ever saw. They were finally persuaded to lay their pistols and the money on the table in charge of chosen friends; the door was locked and a messenger was dispatched five miles in the country to bring Colonel _____, a noted local celebrity—a planter who stood high in social as well as sporting circles. We waited three hours; he came, and after hearing the testimony gave the pile to "old rough and ready," and Captain R____ yielded gracefully, a wiser but a poorer man.

After dinner a stranger named Peck gave me a letter to carry across the river and also enough tobacco to smoke me to Natchez. I loafed about until the steamboat started at 5 o'clock in the afternoon; took passage in her to Trinity, costing me $15 besides transportation furnished by the Confederate States. I am now on boat enjoying the beautiful scenery on the river; wish my dear wife was here to participate in my pleasure; such a sunset! It is a vision for a poet.

Tuesday, MAY 5th.

Yesterday evening there were heavy clouds and a good deal of lightning in the North; after supper laid down on the deck and slept very comfortable until awakened by a heavy rain; gathered up my blanket and crowded into the state room, which proved to be almost suffocating. I was very sleepy, so went down in the engine room and slept until morning, crosswise on two barrels of rum; waked up quite refreshed to enjoy the beautiful scenery on the banks of the Ouachita, among the most picturesque of which was a high bluff on which was a single grave; a romantic lady, the wife of a pilot, was buried there by her request, where her gentle spirit might keep vigil over the destinies of her husband. We stopped during the morning to take an old rail fence for fuel; a soldier shot a hog, which gave us fresh pork for dinner; found some very nice mulberries on shore and wished my children, little Stark and Mary, had some of them. Had a very pleasant trip on to Hamburg; went ashore there and got transportation to Trinity; after supper proceeded down to the river and met the steamer, *Tucker*; stopped and had a talk and got the Natchez Courier.

Forgot to say above that I met Dr. Rock on this steamer; learned from him that Lieutenant Brandon was at Pine Bluff on the 8th of April, and was going to Virginia. Dr. Rock is on his way to Richmond. We reached Trinity about 12 o'clock at night, on Tuesday, the 5th, and have not stopped long enough during the day to write up this diary, and at night had no light; left the Trinity in a skiff with five others; proceeded up the Ouachita for about six miles; then into Brushy Bayou; after following this for about two miles the thorns and bushes were so troublesome that we had to get to land and walk about four miles, while the negroes worked the skiff through. In this walk I got far enough ahead of the skiff to take a nap; laid down on the ground and slept gloriously for an hour; would have enjoyed it more with a blanket to lie on. At the end of this walk we had a very good breakfast by paying five dollars a dozen for some eggs and furnishing our own coffee, and then paying two dollars a piece for breakfast. After breakfast pulled the skiff overland into Cane Bayou, and proceeded up this for six miles to Turtle Lake, a beautiful sheet of water three miles long; from this we entered Cocoda Bayou, which we followed for eight miles into Concordia Lake, up which we rowed for seven or eight miles, which landed us about three miles from Natchez. All this skiff trip is through just such a country as an alligator would thrive in; affording fine facilities for fishing and duck shooting; no one but a Newfoundland dog would enjoy it. We procured a cart to take our baggage to the Mississippi river; crossed in a skiff to Natchez; remained there all night and left Thursday morning for Brookhaven; stopped at Dr. Holden's and got the second good dinner I have had since I left home; reached McDaniel's at dark and found it quite a nice place, and met here that rare creature of the West—an old maid; she seems to be quite a nice person and I think has been doomed to this state of single felicity by circumstances for which she is not responsible. We got a good breakfast at 4 o'clock in the morning, which enabled us to reach Brookhaven (where I am now writing) by 10 o'clock. On the road to this place I passed a bridge which Grierson's Cavalry had destroyed, and here I see the remains of the depot which they burned. These are the first practical examples of Yankee vandalism I have seen during the war. I expect to leave here today at 2 o'clock. Reached Jackson at 6 o'clock and found the train for Meridian about to start and had no time to get transportation, and so have to remain here against my will until tomorrow evening. All these days which I have been delayed I had hoped to spend in Columbia, South Carolina.

Sunday, MAY 10th.

On the cars between Meridian and Selma tried to get transportation at Jackson to Augusta, but the quartermaster declined to give it to me; took it to Atlanta and will try to get it to Augusta from there. Left Jackson at 6 o'clock yesterday evening; Greggs' Brigade had just come in from Port Hudson; met several regiments at Meridian going to Vicksburg and to the fortifications between Vicksburg and Jackson; reached Meridian at 3:30 a.m. and floundered about the depot until 5 o'clock and got a pretty good breakfast for a dollar and a half, and started at 6 o'clock for Selma; reached the landing at 11 o'clock; had a tedious time changing baggage and then only went four miles up the river to Demopolis and went through another tedious lugging of baggage from one point to another, and finally sat in the cars for an hour and a half bored and hungry; got off at last and went rattling through beautiful fields of corn nearly all the way to Selma; took the steamer *Cherokee* from Montgomery and am now on my way up the river, and, Oh! what would I not give to have Mary and the children with me now, for the route is comparatively easy from here to Columbia.

Monday; MAY 11th.

Reached Montgomery this afternoon about 5:30, just too late for the cars, hence must be detained another night on the road. I walked up town a little while ago and met Mr. John A. Elmore; inquired about Culp, my old college chum, and found he was a lieutenant in the army at Vicksburg; his family is with his father-in-law. Heard here of "Stonewall" Jackson's death; it is a sad calamity for the south, but I doubt not God will raise up other great spirits to aid us with their counsels and to fight our battles for us. I wrote a letter on the steamboat, which I intended to hand to someone to mail across the Mississippi, or else mail it in Augusta.

Wednesday, MAY 13th.

Left Montgomery in a crowded train of cars; when we reached the coal station found a suspicious personage, of whom the guard took charge; he had no papers and said he was a substitute for a nephew of Dr. Green, of Fort Valley, and that his papers were in possession of a squad who had left him at Montgomery, he having some other friends there, and becoming too convivial to leave. He said he had paid a policeman one hundred dollars to let him out and then walked to the coal station. I wrote a letter for him to Dr. Green, explaining the circumstance and askings his assistance. This little affair gave the curious some excitement.

About the time I reached West Point a gentleman named J. J. Thrasher, of Atlanta, introduced himself and made inquiries about Mrs. Nelson, wife of Col. Allison Nelson, or "Mary," as he affectionately termed her. He seemed to know all about the family and gave me their history and said their father, Mr. Green, was one of his best friends. He also asked after Mr. Knight; spoke very highly of him and said that his father, his uncles and aunts, Mr. and Mrs. Mangum and Avery, had all died within the last three months.

I gradually became sociable enough with Mr. Thrasher and his daughter to enjoy their lunch very much, the first delicacies of the kind that I have seen since I left Texas.

Soon afterwards a very kind old gentleman named John A. Broughton asked me to take a seat by him, and informed me that he had once been to Texas and farmed in Fayette county, but concluded to return. He is about the third man I have met who was ever able to get away from Texas after being once fixed there. He is, however, worth a million of dollars and has only two children. He offered me money and divided his lunch with me. I parted with him at Madison about 12 o'clock at night.

The cars being very much crowded, I offered a neat looking person a seat by me. He seemed to be very communicative, and gave me a full history of his experiments in distilling, and of his daughter's progress at Northern schools, which he greatly preferred to Southern. He told me his name was ____, and that he was a first cousin of Judge ____, of ____ in Texas, whom I know very well. He gave me a very minute account of the circumstances under which the Judge left Georgia. It amounted in substances to this: The Judge took part and assisted an editor in writing a very scurrilous article, commenting on the conduct of a state senator, Mr. ____. The senator was offended and was about to call the editor to account for the article, when the editor shot and killed him, and Judge ____ left because he feared that his testimony would convict his friend. My informant added further that it was thought by some that the trial would develop facts which might show Judge ____ to be accessory to the killing, etc. This entire circumstance, of which I had heard vague and indefinite rumors in Texas, was related to me voluntarily, without a hint on my part that I had ever heard of it before, and without a question to draw him out particularly on the subject. He seemed to be very candid and loquacious on all subjects, and gave me a very minute history of his own domestic affairs.

31

COLUMBIA, SOUTH CAROLINA, MAY 16th.

The date of May 13th was written at the depot in Augusta, Georgia, and brings me to my arrival at that place. I had intended passing on without delay, but heard from a stranger on the cars that Lieutenant Selman and my other Texas friends were at Montgomery and would be in Augusta on the next train. This determined me to spend a day in Augusta, to let them overtake me. I had my baggage carried to the Augusta Hotel, and after making myself presentable, called at Mr. Carter's drug store and found that he had gone to Charleston to purchase a new supply of drugs. I met at the drug store Mr. Rogers, a brother of Mrs. Hardin, and who looks very much like her; spent an hour inquiring for Mr. Robert Lamar, my wife's uncle, then walked around to Dr. Ford's; found Miss Sadie May and Mrs. Clinch sitting in the passage; they did not recognize me and asked me to walk into the parlor. I found Dr. Ford and a patient in consultation. He seemed delighted to see me. I went into the breakfast table, and when the ladies found me out I was plied with questions about my wife and the children, and must say here, once for all—"nunc pro tunc"—that I have spent the last three days in a like agreeable task. My sweet wife seems to be beloved by everyone who knows her. I stayed but a short time and learned that Mr. Clinch was mayor at Vicksburg and De Saussure Ford was with Bragg's army. I went to Mr. Barney Dunbar's once and had a long talk with him; went out to Mr. Robert Lamar's and there found that grandma and Aunt Mary were absent. When I arrived at Columbia and Augusta depot, met Lieutenant Selman, Mullens and Burwell Aycock, who had left me sick at Marshall, Texas. Aycock went to Chattanooga on account of old wounds still troubling him. After the trials and difficulties of our trip and our

32

unpleasant separation, our meeting was a joyful occasion. They went on to Weldon and I came on to Columbia, not, however, without a serious loss—my blankets were stolen out of the cars at Branchville.

I reached Columbia, at 6 o'clock a.m., and went up to Major Stark's without giving any notice. Decca Stark was just about to start to Fairfield. She exclaimed, "I do believe it is Mr. West," and then both looked blank until I smiled. They thought that Mary and the children must be dead, but matters were soon explained. I took breakfast with the family, and after spending the morning in giving a full account of myself and Mary, went up town; met John McDowell, from Camden; he is captain of a mounted rifle company from Montgomery, Alabama.

After dinner I walked out to Stark's Hill to see aunties; found them all looking well, especially Aunt Mac. The garden was looking beautiful; indeed, old Columbia altogether is the handsomest place I ever saw, and I think if my Mary was with me now I would be perfectly happy. Everyone here has received me so joyfully; both Mary's friends and my own have met me so cordially that I cannot be otherwise than happy, and mother and Decca have done, and seem willing to do, so much for my comfort that I feel willing to make any sacrifice for my wife to share these attentions with me. Mary is more entitled to all this pleasure than I am; but fortune dispenses favors in an inexplicable manner. I trust my wife may be here before I return to Texas. She shall not be tied down in the creek bottom forever.

On the second day I walked out to Aunt Carrie Stark's, in company with Decca. She did not know who had called and primped up as if she expected to meet a stranger. She was delighted to see me and seemed very cheerful; introduced us to Mrs. Raoul and Mrs. Hamilton. After I started out she came into the portico with

me and her manner was entirely changed; she spoke of
her afflictions and seemed very sad. God has dealt very
severely with her, and I pray to be delivered from such
visitations, unless it be for my good, which I cannot believe. Heaven will not try me thus. We came on to Mrs.
Elmore's and saw Mrs. Elmore, Miss Cornelia and Miss
Grace; Mrs. Elmore and Miss Cornelia look five years
younger than they did five years ago. We came on to
the city and went to the deguerrean gallery to have a
copy made of Mary's picture. Decca Stark is with me in
all these visits, and seems willing to do anything for my
enjoyment.

On the third day of my stay I spent the morning at
home with Decca and mother. In the afternoon Decca
and I walked to Sydney park and over it; saw not a soul
whom we recognized. The park is wonderfully improved,
and shows what energy and taste can do in a little while.
There is some encouragement and satisfaction to exercise taste and energy in a country where it rains; there
is none in Texas.

We called at Dr. William Reynolds' on the way home.
They are living now at the old Muller place, and have
improved it vastly. Misses Jane and Sophia Reynolds
have a very large school, and Mrs. Reynolds superin-
tends the housekeeping and the comfort of the board-
ers, of whom they have a large number. Miss Jane was
sick, but Mrs. Reynolds and Miss Sophia and Miss So-
phy Niel received me very joyfully. I met here two of old
Dr. DeLeon's daughters from Columbia. All parties were
anxious to hear of my Aunt Catherine Eccles and of the
other children. Part of the improvement consists in the
removal of the exclusive-looking, tall plank fence, which
is replaced by an iron railing. The flower garden is tastily arranged and there is generally an inviting air about
the entire premises. A graduate will not look back upon

the place as an escaped convict views and remembers the penitentiary.

The fourth day of my stay in Columbia was Sunday. I attended the Baptist church in the morning and in the evening and the Episcopal in the afternoon. The Baptist meeting house is quite handsomely finished and does credit to the taste of the denomination here. There is also in it a magnificent organ, said to be the finest in the city. Its tones are grand and full, and it certainly adds greatly to the beauty and solemnity of the worship and services. The building will seat comfortably over two thousand persons.

On Monday, the fifth day, I took breakfast with Major Stark, at 6 o'clock in the morning, and walked with him out to the farm and over it. A place with such water privileges would be invaluable in Texas. Vegetables of every description could be had all the year round. I looked at the overseer's house and the well so close, the garden and the chicken yard, and thought how happy and blest Mary would be if she were there. Ought we to return to South Carolina? Oh, for light and direction on this subject! Have I the right to debar a pure, good woman from all the endearments and joys of home, because she loves me and is ready and willing to make any sacrifice for me? I returned home by Stark's Hill and took breakfast with aunties, and had a pleasant visit. Aunt Mary gave me a very nice blanket with which to replace my lost one. I came by Mrs. Singleton's and stayed an hour; made the acquaintance of Captain Haskell, who seems to be a very gentlemanly and sensible person; think I would like him very much on further acquaintance.

Came home and walked up town with Major Stark to see about having my transportation changed so as to permit me to go to Charlotte instead of going back to Kingsville. Mr. J. Pringle Smith seemed very willing to accommodate me, but exhibited a very laudable disposition to avoid any violation of duty or law. He finally required me to pay my own way for fifty miles on the road, this being the difference between the distances from Kingsville to Weldon and from Columbia to Weldon.

In returning to Major Stark's I met Mr. Lem Boykin, son of Mr. Burwell Boykin. He is captain of a company on the coast, and is as wild and "harum scarum" as ever. After dinner I received a visit from Mr. Breaker, the Baptist minister, and his wife. He is a sensible man and she is a pretty woman. Of course such company is always pleasant.

I walked with Decca to the daguerrean gallery; got the copy of my Mary's picture; am only tolerably pleased with it, but doubt not it will console me in some degree in the long, weary hours I must be away from her. Perhaps I may never see her again until she is a radiant angel in the skies; and I trust in God that whatever other punishment or destiny may await me for my shortcomings in this life, that I may not be shut out from the light of my Mary's face forever. To me there will be but one other countenance in heaven to compare with it and divide my worship—my mother's!

From the window of the daguerrean gallery we witnessed the parade of the Arsenal cadets. They presented an unusually fine appearance and will doubtless do good service in this war during the next five years.

We made a call at Mr. DeSaussure's, but did not find Mrs. Wallace and Mrs. Burroughs at home. Mr. William DeSaussure is the only person except myself who has not forgiven me for leaving Mary in Texas. We called at Mr. Shand's on the way home, but Mrs. Wilson was out. We returned after tea and had a pleasant visit of an hour.

I forgot to say that Decca went with me to see old Mrs. Murphy after service on Sunday afternoon. The old lady was in bed, severely stricken with the palsy, but seemed animated and bright on my entrance, and talked of Mary and the pleasant times she had with her "in this very room." She seemed very much distressed to know that her grandson and only heir was an orphan in the hands of his mother's people, the Catholics.

Thus I have brought this hurried journal down to Tuesday morning, May the 19th, at which time I am sitting in the parlor alone, and have been for an hour, waiting for mother and Decca to get up for breakfast. I have very few general comments to make on my visit; suffice it to say, that I am agreeably surprised to find that the degree of pleasure I have enjoyed in this short visit has exceeded ten-fold my anticipations. I did not think that I would receive such a hearty welcome and so much kindness. I owe it all to Mary and have regretted and still regret that I did not make the effort to bring her with me notwithstanding the difficulties and uncertainties of the route. I received the following memorandum today, to wit: Miss Nannie Norton, corner of Eighth and Marshall Streets, Richmond, Va.; T. Lamar Stark, Edgefield Hussars; Captain Clark, Second Regiment S.C.V. Cavalry; Colonel Butler, Hampton's Brigade, Va.

Wednesday, MAY 20th.

I spent yesterday morning writing to my precious wife. I wrote two letters; one to take the chances and uncertainties of the mails; the other reserved until I can find someone going across the Mississippi River. I called on Mrs. Bachman and there met Mrs. Carroll and her daughter. Mrs. Bachman spoke of Mary as of a sister; she is a sweet, good woman and was anxious to do something for my comfort. She gave me a letter to Captain Bachman and also one for some of her cousins in Virginia; wanted me to leave all my extra clothing with Miss Nannie Norton in Richmond; said that Wat Taylor had left his things there. Mrs. Bachman's paintings are enchanting to me. What a useful and delightful accomplishment painting is. By it we can leave such precious and enduring mementos of ourselves, when all other memories have faded in the oblivion of a shadowy past. I spent the afternoon with mother only, and began to feel like I had somebody to love me this side of the Mississippi. For all that I hold dearest is west of the river. Mother (Mrs. Stark) has treated me as her own son. She has furnished me with clothing, which I needed; has given me $40.00 and appears anxious to do more for me. I went out to auntie's, at Stark Hill, late in the afternoon and bade them goodbye; talked as if they were parting with one who had a right to their affections; all this nerves me very much and added to the approval of my own conscience makes me more willing and ready to suffer whatever may be in store for me and let my trials be what they may. May God save my wife and children from affliction. Let all the evil which may perchance be in store for them be meted out to me. After supper last night mother went upstairs with me and we concluded that it would be best to carry only a change of clothing and leave the rest in Columbia with her, to be sent as I needed them. She packed my things and spoke so kindly and affectionately to me that I love her next to Mary. It is now 6 o'clock on Wednesday morning. I am waiting for Decca to get ready to go to the depot with me; she is going as far as Winsboro to pay a visit to Jennie Preston Means.

Thursday, MAY 21st.

I left with Decca Stark. There was no incident worth mentioning between Columbia and Winsboro. We met Stark Means at the depot. He is in fine health and only limping a little from his wound. Chester, Charlotte and Raleigh all larger and more city-like than I expected. We passed Concord and Salisbury at night. It is twenty years since last I saw any of them, and my sweet mother was present then. I was a boy nine years old. I recollected leaving a whip on the mantelpiece of the Charlotte Hotel at that time, and I have never forgotten it. Mr. Crist, at Gott's Hotel, in Salem, made this whip for me. I am now at Raleigh, and since I am separated with my friends (perhaps forever) I wish I was with old Company E.

Friday, MAY 22nd.

Left Raleigh about 9 o'clock yesterday morning. The road from Raleigh to Weldon is the most crooked and through the most broken country I ever saw. Every foot of it is over an embankment or through a deep cut. The land along the route is all poor and barren and yet there are some beautiful residences and the people seem to be doing well. How they live I cannot tell. There were occasionally fine apple orchards and clover fields. I had the good fortune to meet up with Mr. Carpenter, a member of the North Carolina legislature. He was a pleasant companion and had some genuine whiskey, having married the heiress of a distiller. I made also the acquaintance of an old gentleman named Miller, who was on his way to Richmond to see two wounded nephews, one of whom had lost an arm; he also had some whiskey, which he said came from the drug store and must be good. He had also some cakes, good ham and fresh butter, which I enjoyed very much. He is a Baptist and is acquainted with Mr. Lemmond, of Waco, Texas. We reached Weldon about 5 o'clock in the afternoon, and as the cars were not to start until 9 o'clock, I concluded to take a stroll. I obtained a drink of the coldest water I ever drank and observed the address of Captain H. A. Troutman on a box, which put me on the lookout for him. I soon met him and we had a long talk on old college times. He had married a Miss Napier. John Neely is dead; Miss Lou is married to Ed McClure. Billy Clifton has become a devout Baptist. Charley Boyd, John McLemore and Lucius Gaston are all killed, murdered by fanatical vandals; ten thousand mercenaries cannot pay for such men as these. They helped to make and adorn the character of a noble people. They were all my college friends. We loved each other and cherished common hopes of a happy future.

I went to supper with Troutman. He boards with the post commissary, who, of course, gets a little of everything. We had light rolls, scrambled eggs, genuine coffee, salmon, etc,, for supper. The commissary is run by Mr. Peterson, brother of Judge Peterson, of San Antonio, Texas. We left Weldon at 9 o'clock and jogged along slowly until about 3 o'clock a.m., when we reached Petersburg. I shouldered my carpet-bag, overcoat and blanket and walked a mile to the depot. Cars left Petersburg about 5 o'clock a.m., and ran so slowly that I had ample time to inspect the country. When we came within eight miles of Richmond I observed a large amount of timber felled on either side of the road and fortifications thrown up to prevent the advance of the Yanks. When we came within three miles of Richmond one of the bars which connects the cars broke, and we were detained for half an hour or more, but another engine very opportunely came up behind us and pushed us on to Richmond. I found it a much more beautiful place than I had anticipated. The scenery in crossing James River is especially attractive. I put up at the American Hotel and spent the day in wandering "up and down" and "going to and fro" in it. I called on Miss Wigfall, Mrs. Chestnut, Miss Nannie Norton (who was absent), Miss Mary Fisher, Mr. and Mrs. Barnwell and met there Mrs.

Carter. Called at the Cabinet Quarters and delivered to C. S. Senator Hon. James Chestnut, a letter (from Hon. Guy M. Bryan, of Texas) to the president. I went to the Ballard House to see Hon. H. P. Brewster, of Texas; was unable to find him. Delivered Mr. Carter's letter to Mr. Winston, who was too busy to notice me, so I retired. I gave him also the letter to Mrs. Benton. Dined with Colonel and Mrs. Chestnut, in company with Billy Preston, who is now major of artillery. Had fish and corn bread, rice and lettuce for dinner, with iced whiskey to wash it down. After dinner went to the Spotswood Hotel, met Captain Rice and Jimmy Winn, also Minnie Moses, whom I have not seen for eight years. He is a clerk in some of the departments. I returned to Miss Mary Fisher's in the afternoon and left my overcoat in her charge. I am too tired to make comments, though I have seen a great deal to write about. I am writing this in the public room of the American Hotel about 11 o'clock at night. They have charged me $7.50 for supper, night's lodging and breakfast.

Sunday, MAY 24th.

Left Richmond yesterday about 6:30 o'clock a.m. Found a number of the Texas Brigade and a few of my regiment on the cars and soon became acquainted with them. The trip was monotonous, as usual, until we reached Gordonsville, where the crowd was so great that twenty of us had to stand on the platform. General J.E.B. Stuart was aboard and appeared to be very fond of ladies and flowers. He is of medium size, well formed, fair complexion, blue eyes, whiskers and mustache of sun-burnt reddish color, usually accompanying fair skin. I had quite a pleasant time on the platform watching the attempts of the proscribed to get a seat in the cars and their repulse by the provost guard. The cars were for the accommodation of ladies and commissioned officers. I

41

never knew soldiers of any grade to be put in the same category with women before. I happened, however, to meet Tom Lipscomb, my old college classmate, who is now a major, who managed to get me in under his wing. We had a long talk about Columbia and old college days. He informed me that Lamar Stark, my wife's brother, was a prisoner confined in the old capitol in Washington City.

We reached Mitchell's Station at 4 o'clock p.m.; walked five miles, a hot walk, to camp on the Rapidan, near Raccoon Ford. My regiment, the Fourth Texas, has a delightful camping place in a grove of large chestnut trees, on a hillside. We have no tents and the ground is hard and rocky, but we are all satisfied, and one day's observation has led me to believe that no army on earth can whip these men. They may be cut to pieces and killed, but routed and whipped, never! I called on Colonel B. F. Carter this morning and had quite a pleasant interview. He is a calm, determined man, and one of the finest officers in the division. Today was the regular time for inspection and review. One barefooted and ragged hero came to Colonel Carter's Tent with the inquiry, "Colonel, do you want the barefooted men to turn out today?" to which the Colonel replied negatively, with a smile. I went out to the review which took place in an open field about 600 yards from camp. There were some ladies on horseback on the field. Their presence was cheering and grateful. They were all dressed in black, as were more than two-thirds of the women in the Confederacy. On returning to camp I called on Major Bass, of the First Texas, and gave him $25.00, which I had received for him from Lieutenant Ochiltree, at Shreveport, Louisiana, to be handed to Bass if I did not need it.

I received two haversacks today, miserably weak and slazy, made of thin cotton cloth. I have only taken a change of underwear, towel, soap and Bible and Milton's "Paradise Lost." I have sent all the rest to Richmond with my carpet sack, to be left at Mrs. Mary E. Fisher's, on Franklin street, halfway between Sixth and Seventh.

I wrote a letter to mother and one to wife today and read the 104th Psalm. I opened to it by chance, and it contained just what I felt.

Thursday, MAY 28th.

While we are encamped life is so monotonous that I do not usually regard it as necessary to keep a diary, but occasionally we have a little variety and spice which is exciting and pleasant. Yesterday we received notice early in the morning to prepare to march five miles to attend a review of our division which was to take place about a mile beyond General Hood's headquarters. We left our camp about 8 o'clock a.m. and reached the muster ground about 10 o'clock. We found the artillery posted on the extreme right about three-quarters of a mile from our regiment.

The brigades—Anderson's, Laws', Robertson's and Benning's, were drawn up in line of battle, being over a mile long; our regiment a little to the left of the center. As we were properly formed General Hood and staff galloped down the entire length of the line in front and back again in the rear, after which he took his position about 300 yards in front of the center. The whole division was then formed into companies, preceded by the artillery of about twenty pieces; passed in review before the General, occupying about an hour and a march of over two miles and a half for each company before reaching its original position. The spectacle was quite imposing and grand, and I wish Mary and the children could see such a sight. After passing in review we rested awhile and were then again placed in line of battle, and the artillery divided into two batteries, came out on opposite hills in front of us, where they practiced half an hour or more with blank cartridges. This was the most exciting scene of the day except the one which immediately followed, viz: We were ordered to fix bayonets and the whole line to charge with a yell, and sure enough I heard and joined in the regular Texas war whoop. This was the closing scene of the day, after which we marched back to camp. There was an immense crowd of citizens out on the occasion as spectators, reminding me very much of an old time South Carolina review.

On our return to camp Companies E and F were ordered on picket guard about a mile and a half from camp. We packed up everything and were soon off and are now encamped on the bank of the Rapidan at Raccoon Ford. Last night was quite cool but I slept comfortably after the tramp of yesterday.

Today Companies E and F are variously employed. There is one squad fishing, another has made a drag of brush and are attempting to catch fish by the wholesale. Two or three other squads are intensely interested in games of poker; some are engaged on the edge of the water washing diverse soiled garments as well as their equally soiled skins. I belonged to this latter class for a while, and have spent the remainder of the morning watching the varying success or failure of the fishermen and poker-players, and in reading a few chapters and Psalms in the Old Testament and the history of the crucifixion in the New. I forgot to say that on yesterday I met on the parade ground Captain Wade and Major Cunningham, of San Antonio, and also John Darby and Captain Barker. Darby is the chief surgeon of Hood's Division. I went up to a house today about half a mile from our picket camp and found a negro woman with some corn bread and buttermilk. A friend who was with me gave her a dollar for her dinner, which we enjoyed very much. The woman was a kind-hearted creature and looked at me very sympathetically, remarking that I did not look like I was used to hard work, and that I was a very nice looking man to be a soldier, etc., etc.

Here are the chapters I have read today: Deut., 23:14; II Chron., 32:8; Jeremiah, 49:2; Revelation, 21 :14.

Sunday, MAY 31st.

This morning about daylight we received orders to be ready to march at 8:30. All is bustle now getting ready. I have been to the spring for water and have just returned; have read the 52nd chapter of Isaiah, and 35th Psalm; am now about to pack up.

Sunday evening at sunset.—We have marched about fourteen miles today—a hot dusty march. Nothing of interest occurred. We are now bivouacked in a pine grove twenty miles from Fredericksburg, with our arms stacked with orders to be ready to leave at a moment's notice. The march has not fatigued me anything like as much as many hunts I have taken at home. Some friend of the soldiers has been kind enough to send us a number of religious papers, and I am now enjoying the "Christian Observer," published at Richmond.

Monday, JUNE 1st.

Received orders to retrace our steps and marched fourteen miles over the same dusty road and are now camped in two miles of Raccoon Ford. I am pretty tired and my feet very much blistered. Our clever, hospitable steward gave me a toddy and let me have a basin to wash my feet in. Our camp is an oak grove with thick undergrowth. There seems to be as many spiders as leaves. They tickle me very much crawling over my face. I ate my last ration of meal and will be without tomorrow.

Thursday, JUNE 4th.

On yesterday evening we received orders to cook three days' rations and be ready to march today at daylight. We were up late at night cooking and left this morning early, wading the Rapidan at Raccoon Ford. We are now, 2 o'clock p.m., one mile from Culpepper Court House, having marched fifteen miles this morning.

Saturday, JUNE 6th.

On yesterday we marched six miles to a large open field beyond Culpepper to witness a review of General Stuart's cavalry. There were 8,000 or 10,000 horsemen covering an immense area. The infantry were permitted to rest and gaze at will, from the railroad embankment, on their maneuvers. Except the difference in the numbers present there was nothing to note which may not be seen at the review of a regiment. The great numbers inspired a feeling of awe and created an impression of strength and security.

We returned to camp about sunset, having made a march of twelve miles for recreation, entertainment and inspiration. Just as I was writing the last line we received orders to be ready to march at 12 o'clock; it is now nearly 11. I asked yesterday for Lamar Stark, but I learned from Wat Taylor that he was across the river so I cannot tell when I shall see him.

Monday, JUNE 8th.

On the morning of the 6th, Saturday, we were ordered to be prepared to march at 12 o'clock. We started about 1 o'clock towards the Rappahanock. It rained in the afternoon, and I was soaked to the skin, and the road very muddy. We dragged along until 10 o'clock at night and were then ordered to camp without fires. We slept on the wet ground in a perfect heap; 10,000 or 12,000 men lying promiscuously on the side of a public road, like so many tired hounds, was a novel sight, or rather sound, to me. I slept soundly, except when waked up by the rain falling in my face. At daylight on Sunday morning we were ordered to form and were marched back over the same road to our camp near Culpepper, a distance of sixteen miles. We remained there until morning, when we moved to this place, about half a mile farther from Culpepper. This marching and counter-marching is what the military authorities call making a demonstration. It is a tiresome and monotonous business, but if it accomplishes the purpose for which I left home I will be satisfied.

Tuesday, JUNE 9th.

This morning about six o'clock there was heavy cannonading towards the Rappahanock. It is now after nine o'clock and the firing still continues. We have just received orders to form and are now resting in line ready to move at the word of command. Perhaps I may see my first battle today or tomorrow—will it be the last?

Saturday, JUNE 13th.

Went yesterday to call on General Kershaw. Found Henry Deas, Albert Doby and Charley Dunlap at his headquarters. Neddy Dunlap is foragemaster; Tom Salmon, surgeon; Jimmy Davis is adjutant of DeSaussure's Fifteenth Regiment South Carolina Volunteers. John Kennedy is Colonel of a regiment; Jim Villepigue, quartermaster; Frank Gilliard, major. Josie Dunlap is in William Shannon's old company, of which Doby is now captain. Tom Chestnut is captain of a cavalry company. All the above names are old acquaintances and schoolmates of Camden, South Carolina.

(The foregoing pages are copied from diary kept up to June 13th, 1863. Here are some letters written to my wife covering a part of the same time as the diary.)

LETTER No. I.
ON THE RAPIDAN, MAY 20, 1863

MY PRECIOUS WIFE:

I am at last safely encamped with the Fourth Texas Regiment in a beautiful grove of chestnut on a hillside about one mile from Raccoon Ford on the Rapidan about seventy-five or eighty miles from Richmond, and must say that I feel better and happier and of a clearer conscience than since the war commenced.

We have no tents and few blankets, mine being lost, you know, and being replaced by a light one which Aunt Mary Stark gave me. The ground is hard but the weather is pleasant and water fine.

I did not believe I could feel so well satisfied so far from you, but, thank God, that I have a full and perfect faith on one point, viz: that whatever may await me, heaven will protect you and the children. I have not felt uneasy for a moment on that subject, and this morning I took out my Bible and opened it by chance and found the (104th) one hundred and fourth Psalm on the mighty power and providence of God. Can you not trust in such a power and enjoy yourself and feel satisfied? I do not want you to be sad a moment on my account.

I am perfectly well and have bacon, bread and a clear conscience. I have consummated the desire of my heart in connecting myself with this brigade. I intend to remain with it until it returns to Texas under a reign of peace, or I expect not to return at all. All of the Waco boys are well except Allen Killingsworth. I am afraid he is dangerously sick. He was in the hospital a month ago and came out too soon. He has a high fever and flux and is very weak this morning.

Billy Dunklin and all the rest are well. We have been encamped at this place for a week and may be ordered to move at any moment. I knew everything the brigade was doing when I was at home and on the way here, but am unable to find out anything about it now. We know less than anybody else. Tom Williams is the same old Tom. The whole brigade is in fine spirits, and it really does seem strange to see men who have lost so many friends seem so careless and happy. They sometimes talk almost like bullies at a street corner, except with a mild, calm air of determination and no swagger. The usual feeling seems to be, "We can't be whipped, but we may all be killed." I am satisfied that an imprudent leader could carry them to destruction.

I met Tom Lipscomb yesterday on the cars. He is a major in Hampton's Brigade, in Butler's Regiment. Your brother, Lamar Stark, has been scouting in the enemies lines for more than six months. A few days ago he got into a fight; he was captured and Gillespie Thornwell was killed. Lamar is now a prisoner in the Old Capitol at Washington. Some of them have been exchanged already by lot, but Lamar was not drawn. He is well treated and will doubtless be exchanged soon. I learned this from Lipscomb, who got it from returned prisoners so do not despond about him.

If you ever get my letter in which I make some suggestions about your coming to Columbia, you must let them be qualified by any change in the condition of our affairs in the West. Leave the servants by all means, all of them, and do not go more than $500.00 in debt. If you try it, write to me from Jackson, Mississippi. As soon as I get too sick to march or get wounded I will come to Columbia. You and Bro. Burleson, Mrs. Pearre, Miss Lambden, Dr. McDonald and Mrs. Carter must pray for me.

Your husband, faithfully ever,

JOHN C. WEST.

LETTER No. II.
CAMP ON THE RAPIDAN, MAY 25, 1863

MY PRECIOUS WIFE:

I have written to you by every opportunity I have had since I left home, and have sent letters by mail and by individuals. I wrote to you yesterday by mail and today I am writing again because Mr. Robertson, of Texas, in our company, is going home on sixty days furlough and will take the letter to Waco. My letters are in substance pretty much the same because I felt so uncertain about your getting them that I repeated things which I was anxious for you to know; so you must not think that I am especially "exercised" on a particular subject of any character because it is mentioned in successive letters. We are camped in a beautiful grove of large chestnut trees on a hillside, about a mile from Raccoon Ford. We have no tents and the ground is hard and a little rocky. My fine blanket and shawl were stolen between Branchville and Columbia.

I have left my overcoat with Miss Mary E. Fisher, Franklin Street, between Sixth and Seventh, at Richmond, and all of my other effects, except a change of clothing, at Columbia; and since I have come to camp and gotten a haversack (there are no knapsacks) I have taken out one suit of underwear and put all my remaining effects in my carpetsack to be sent to Richmond; so you see my load is quite light. You need never trouble yourself to send me anything but letters and cheerful hopes. We cannot fight and carry baggage, and my supply will last for three years with what mother can send me. It is no use to have clothes which must be thrown away on every march. We are now about to change our camp and have four days rations cooked, but do not know what we are to do or where to go.

I saw Tom Lipscomb yesterday. He is a major in Hampton's Brigade. He told me that Lamar Stark was taken prisoner in the same fight in which Gillespie Thornwell was killed. Some of them have been exchanged and Lamar will soon be. He is being well treated. This is reported by some of the exchanged prisoners. All of the Waco boys are well except Allen Killingsworth. He has been very dangerously sick with flux and high fever. He is not altogether out of danger but a great deal better. We are trying to find a private house for him as we are to leave here today. I have said something in previous letters about your coming to Columbia, and have stated my plans so fully in two letters, one by mail and the other by hand, that I will only say here that if it is as easy for you to get through as when I left you may try it if you choose, but leave *all the servants* at home. You must get a good escort to Jackson, Missisisippi.

I opened my Bible on the first day I arrived at camp, and the first place my eyes fell upon was the 104th Psalm. Cannot a God of such power preserve me and you, or take care of you without me. Be cheerful and do not borrow trouble on my account. I forgot to say that we have plenty of bread and meat and the finest water I ever saw. Today is a chilly, damp day, and it is raining a little. We will sleep wet tonight as there is no way to keep blankets dry. Aunt Mary Stark gave me a blanket in Columbia. Kiss the little darlings for me, and be assured that whatever befalls or awaits me is *all right. God does it and He does all things well.*

Your husband, faithfully ever,

John C. West.

P. S.—John Darby, my old classmate, is our division surgeon, and gives general satisfaction to everyone. He is very much in love with Miss M____ P_____.

51

LETTER No. III.

CAMP ON THE RAPIDAN, MAY 26, 1863

MY PRECIOUS WIFE:

The order to move has been countermanded for the present, and we will be on picket duty for a few days. I wrote you yesterday, thinking it was Tuesday, and that Mr. Robinson would leave today; so I will continue the account of my trip from Columbia. I left there on the 20th in company with Decca Stark, who was about to pay a visit to Mrs. Jennie Preston Means. I found Stark Means at the depot in Winsboro. He is looking very well and his wounds have nearly healed. I found all those up-country villages a great deal larger and more prosperous looking than I expected.

When I reached Weldon I found Troutman there as quartermaster, and spent an hour or two with him very pleasantly, talking over old college days. He has married Miss Napier and seems to be in good circumstances. Miss Lou Neely has married Ed. McClure. John Neely is dead. John McLemore, Lucius Gaston and Charlie Boyd (Capt), have all been killed in battle. The sacrifice of a nation of hired Hessians will not atone for the loss of such men as these. I took supper with Troutman at the commissary's residence, and had a first-rate meal. I reached Richmond on Friday morning about 9 o'clock, and after paying a barber $2.50 for a shave and shampoo I took a stroll over the city; called on Mrs. Wigfall, Mrs. Chestnut, Miss Barnwell, etc., etc., and found all at home except Miss Nannie Norton, whom I also called to see; and I also called on Miss Mary E. Fisher. Miss Nannie was on a visit to Raleigh.

I had a letter from Mrs. Julia Bachman to Miss Fisher. She asked me in and gave me a drink of water, flavored with mint, which was very acceptable. Mrs. Carter, whom I met at Mrs. Darnwell's, seemed very glad to hear from you and asked to be remembered to you. Mr. Barnwell was quite sick. Mrs. Chestnut invited me to dine and Willie Preston to meet me; he is a major of artillery. Jack Preston has married Miss Huger. I delivered Mr. Carter's letter to Mr. Winston, but he had no time to talk to me; he has a task for each day and not a moment to spare. I spent more of my time sightseeing, but was especially interested in the equestrian statue of Washington, which surmounts a plain shaft of marble, with a granite base. There are also on the same monument statues of Jefferson, Mason and Henry. This is in Capitol Square, which is beautifully shaded. The Square is a great resort for all classes in leisure hours. Just at this point I was called out to our company drill, which has given me an hour and a half of good exercise. I must write a letter to some of the folks at Austin; so will have to curtail this. Let me repeat, you must take good care of yourself and not trouble about me. If you cannot manage any other way you must quit thinking of me entirely, except enough to keep from forgetting me altogether. My little picture of you copied from one in Columbia is charming, and is a source of great pleasure to me. Tell the servants to behave well, and to obey you, or I will haunt them. Talk to the children about me every day and tell Stark to say his lessons regularly.

Your husband, faithfully ever,

JOHN C. WEST.

LETTER No. IV.
CAMP ON THE RAPIDAN, MAY 30, 1863

MY PRECIOUS WIFE:

I write you a few lines by an Irishman who has just gotten a discharge from our regiment. I merely write to take the chance of letting you know that I am well and well satisfied. I am afraid that the Irishman will get drunk and lose this, so I have no heart to write you as fully as I would wish, besides I have only a few moments to write in.

We are five miles from the rest of the brigade on picket duty at Raccoon Ford. All of our company are doing well except Allen Killingsworth, who is sick at a private house about five miles off. He is getting better. I have written you a great many letters, and trust that this may reach you safely. Your daguerreotype is a great consolation to me; I look at it every day and remember the 49th Chapter and 11th verse of Jeremiah and feel satisfied, although a letter from home would be a great pleasure to me. I have nothing with me but the clothes on my back and a change of underclothing. I trust that our affairs may so result at Vicksburg as to leave the way open for you to make a visit to Columbia. I have laid out the plan for you in three or four letters. The principal features are for you not to go more than $500.00 in debt, and to leave the servants at home; to get a good escort to Jackson, and as much farther as you can, and then trust to conductors and your own good sense the rest of the way. You need not make or send anything to me as I am unable to march with it, and will have to throw it away. Mother gave me a nice pair of pants; they were cut out and made for $1.50. Lamar was taken prisoner and Gillespie Thornwell killed about three weeks ago. Lamar has been exchanged and is now with his command. Kiss the little darlings for me. I missed the pleasure of seeing Mac in Columbia; she had gone to Charleston. Tell the servants howdy for me, and tell them I say, obey you. Don't forget Stark's lessons.

Your husband, faithfully ever,

JOHN C. WEST.

LETTER No. V.
CAMP CAMP NEAR CULPEPPER, JUNE 8, 1863

MY PRECIOUS WIFE:

I have determined to write you another letter, although I cannot do so with the satisfaction it usually affords me, for I feel so uncertain whether you will ever read what I write.

In this I shall attempt a hurried sketch of the past ten days, unless I am interrupted by an order to leave before I get through. Already, since I have commenced this, we have received notice to be ready to march at the sound of the bugle, which may mean in ten minutes, or ten hours, so you see under what difficulties I write to my sweetheart. On yesterday week we left our camp on the Rapidan, from which I last wrote you, and took a hot and dusty march of sixteen miles towards Fredericksburg, and on the next morning were ordered to retrace our steps and took the same wearisome march and camped near our old ground, where we remained until Thursday morning at daylight, and then proceeded to this place, making another hot and toilsome march of sixteen miles. We remained here until Saturday at 12 o'clock p.m., when we started and marched towards the Rappahannock until 10 o'clock at night. This was a severe march. It rained for two hours in the afternoon and I was completely soaked. It kept drizzling on until daylight. About 10 o'clock at night we were ordered to halt and camp, "without fires," as the Yanks were not far off. It was a novel sight to me to see or rather to hear 20,000 or 30,000 men rushing into the woods on the side of the road to (here comes orders to march at 12 o'clock) secure a place to lie down. We all laid down on "the cold ground" like tired hounds after a chase.

Jim Manahan, Tom Selman and myself laid down together. I was very wet, but very weary. I spent a few minutes listening to the hum of 10,000 tongues cursing the Yankees, talking of home and thinking of how pleasant it would be to take a bath and a toddy, and how sad my wife would feel if she knew all that I was undergoing. I was glad that she did not know it for I did not suffer when I called to mind that these hardships were for the good of my country and the cause of liberty. Amid all this I could not suppress a laugh to hear the expressions of some wayworn chap as a straggler would creep into the bushes and grope about for a place to spread his blanket. I could hear, "get off my hand," "now you are on my foot," "for heaven's sake," (or something worse), "keep your feet out of my face," "Oh, my back, you are right on top of me," "you weigh six hundred pounds," etc., etc.

In the course of an hour all was quiet save the riding back and forth of couriers, which I could hear all night as our "bed" was not more than a foot from the ruts in the road. I could put my hand out in the mud three or four inches deep, but I slept pretty well, and waked at daylight well and heard the order to retrace our steps to our camp near Culpepper. We formed and started back. It was my turn to stand guard, so I was put as part of the rear guard for our regiment, and marched back to this place, which we reached about 2 o'clock yesterday afternoon. I remained on guard until 8 o'clock this morning. I got by the fire a while last night and looked at your daguerreotype by the light of it, and felt happy in the thought of once more meeting you and talking over the dangers which I am now passing through. I feel sure that we shall meet the Yanks in the course of three weeks, but cannot tell when.

All of our movements are inexplicable to me. We never know anything. Even a colonel cannot tell until he starts from camp in which direction he is going, whether North or South. This secrecy is the secret of the success of this army. I forgot to say above, that, as a matter of amusement, and to keep us from getting stiff, we were marched on last Friday six miles off to witness a review of Stuart's cavalry; it was a grand display; 10,000 or 12,000 mounted men is more than I expected to see at one sight. I saw Wat Taylor, but Lamar Stark was off on duty across the river. We returned to camp at night, making twelve miles "for fun" and left the next day at 1 o'clock, as I stated above, so you will see that we have been on the wing for nearly ten days. This marching and countermarching is what they call "Demonstrations," and if they accomplish the objects for which I left my friends I am perfectly satisfied. The marching is no great trouble to me, but twenty or thirty pounds of baggage gets heavy before night, especially in wet weather, on a slippery hillside—when one is so much fatigued that to sneeze or blow his nose jostles him from one side of the road to the other. I saw a great many poor fellows barefooted in the marches of which I have written, but we got some shoes this morning, and I hope we will get on better. Don't forget Stark's lessons and Mary's letters. Kiss them for me and tell the servants howdy. I must stop now and get ready to leave. I hope to hear from you some of these days. I have not received a line yet.

Your husband, faithfully ever,

JOHN C. WEST.

LETTER No. VI.
CAMP NEAR MILLWOOD, TWENTY MILES
WEST OF HARPER'S FERRY, JUNE 23, 1863
To Miss Decca Stark, Columbia, South Carolina

DEAR DECCA:

Yours of the 6th, with one from Miss Nannie Norton of the same date reached me about eight days ago, and I have not had a moment since to answer you, and even now cannot tell whether I shall be interrupted before I am half done with this. I am writing on my knee, with everything packed ready to move at the sound of the bugle. I wrote you last on the 6th of June from near Culpepper Court House. On that day we took a hard march of eighteen miles through the rain, and on very muddy roads. We halted about 10 at night. I was wet and very tired.

There was an order against making fires, as we were near the enemy, being on the same ground on which Stuart fought them a few days afterwards. Of course I slept; a soldier, if he knows his own interest, will sleep whenever opportunity offers, but there were 10,000 or 12,000 men huddled on the side of the road in a promiscuous mass, just as you have seen cattle about a barn lot; no one knowing how much mud or filth he reposed in until the generous light of day revealed it. It rained a good deal during the night and kept me thoroughly soaked. The next morning we were ordered back to the camp near Culpepper, and marched over the same road by 1 o'clock and remained there until the 9th, when early in the morning about 5 o'clock we heard heavy firing of artillery. This was the opening of Stuart's cavalry fight. We formed and marched to Lookout Mountain, about three miles from Stephenburg, and lay in line of battle upon it until the fortune of the day was decided and then returned to camp.

Colonel Frank Hampton was killed in or near Stephenburg by a pistol shot. He was in a hand to hand encounter, it is said. On the 13th we received orders to be ready to march or fight, but it turned out to be only a march of five miles, which we accomplished in an hour and reached Cedar Run, the scene of one of Stonewall Jackson's battles last August. There were a great many unburied skeletons, presenting a very ghastly appearance. There were forty-nine skulls in one little ditch; the bodies were torn to pieces and scattered about, having been taken from their shallow graves by hogs or other animals. A hand or a foot might be seen protruding from the earth, here and there; to mark the last resting place of the patriotic victims of this horrible war.

We left this camp on the 15th and marched through Culpepper towards Winchester. This was one of the hottest days and one of the hottest marches I have yet experienced. Over 500 men fell out by the roadside from fatigue and exhaustion, and several died where they fell; this was occasioned by being overheated and drinking cold water in immoderate quantities, and the enforcement of the order requiring us to wade through creeks and rivers up to our waists without the privilege of even taking off our shoes. I felt quite sick and giddy with a severe pain in my head as I was climbing the hill after wading the Rappahannock, but it passed off, and I kept with the company, though I saw two dead men during the time and several others fall.

Oh! how I would have enjoyed one of mother's mint juleps then as we rested in "the shade of the trees." I slept gloriously that night on a bed of clover and blue grass and thought of the little "pig that lived in clover and when he died he died all over." On the 16th we marched twenty miles without so much suffering, though the day was very warm, and many fell by the way, and like the seed in the parable, "on stony ground," for we were getting towards the mountains. Camped that night near Markham Station in another field of clover, though not so comfortable, for I was very cold and slept little. On the 17th marched fourteen miles up hill and down dale through a beautiful, mountainous region and camped in a splendid grove of oak and hickory about one mile from Upperville, and the neighborhood of some of the most beautiful family mansions I ever saw. All the country we have passed through is perfectly charming, and I cannot see why any Virginian ever leaves Virginia. All that I have seen so far fills my ideal of the "promised land." On the 18th we marched to the Shenandoah, ten miles, and waded it with positive orders not to take off any clothing. The water was deep and cold. I put my cartridge box on my head. The water came to my armpits. We camped about a mile beyond the river. A tremendous rain drenched us before night, so we were reconciled to the wading. My blankets and everything that I had was soaked, except Mary's daguerreotype, which Colonel B. F. Carter took charge of for me. I slept in clothes and blankets soaked wet. On the 19th we marched down the river about ten miles over a very muddy road, and crossed several little streams about knee deep, and then re-crossed the Shenandoah and marched up through Sniggers Gap to the top of the mountain, and here about dark we experienced the hardest storm of wind and rain I ever saw. It seemed to me as if the cold and rain, like the two-edged sword of holy writ, penetrated to the very joints and marrow. I laid down but did not sleep a wink until about an hour before day, and woke up cold and stiff. More than half the soldiers spent the night in a desperate effort to keep the fire burning, which was done with great difficulty.

I took off my clothes, one garment at a time, and dried

them, and baked myself until I felt tolerably well; but truly a soldier knows not what a day may bring forth. Just as I was thoroughly dried, up came another cloud and soaked us again, and then came an order to fall into line "without arms." We were then marched about half a mile from camp and ordered to build a stone fence about half a mile long. This, several thousand men accomplished in about two hours; though it worked me pretty hard to carry and roll stones weighing from 50 to 200 pounds. After my morning's work I dined with Captain Bachman, who had an elegant dinner, consisting mainly of cow-pea soup. After dinner, while we were taking a sociable smoke and chat, an order came to get ready to leave immediately. I hurried to my company and we started back down the mountain, and it was only after getting into the valley, where the sun was shining, that we discovered that we had been encamped in a cloud on the mountain top, right in the heart of the rain factory, the summer resort of Aeolus himself. The division again crossed the Shenandoah, but this time I mounted one of Captain Bachman's caissons and rode over, thus escaping the chill of the waters, though the rain had wet me thoroughly before. I would like for Mrs. Bachman to paint such a scene. It was one of the most splendid for a picture I ever witnessed. 25,000 or 30,000 men, with the wagons and artillery, and horses, all crowding into the stream; a perfect living mass, with towering mountains looking down upon us, and the old stone mill reminding one of the halcyon days of peace and a hundred other incidents which I have not the ability to describe correctly; all united to form one of the most picturesque and wonderful sights my eyes ever beheld.

We camped on this side of the river two nights and one day, and on yesterday morning marched for this place, where for the first time, since the reception of your letter, I have had an opportunity to answer it, for the captain carries my paper for me, and frequently, when we stop, the wagon which carries his baggage is not near to us. I have not written to Mary for ten days, and must ask of you the favor of writing to her for me and giving her the principal items of my journey, for I shall hardly ever get an opportunity of sending a letter by hand from here, and the mails are so uncertain that there is little satisfaction in writing. I am glad she does not know of the privations I am suffering, for it would give her more pain than I have felt in enduring them. I saw Captain Bachman again yesterday. He is well and in fine spirits. I have seen James Davis and all the Camden boys and old friends, and schoolmates in McLaw's division. They each hold an office of some kind They are very lucky in having friends on good terms with the appointing power. I think I could get a place above the ranks, but doubt my qualifications for a higher place. I can march and shoot, and I love my musket next to my wife and my country, and this constitutes my qualifications for military service. I have quite a severe cold, though I am better today than I was yesterday. Don't write this to Mary. I hope we will soon get through our demonstrations and come to the fighting part of the drama.

I have not heard from home yet, though it is more than two months since I left Texas, and there are several letters in the regiment of recent date. I understand there is a large mail for our brigade at the Texas depot, in Richmond, awaiting an opportunity to be sent to us. My love to all, and tell "Theo" to study hard and get his lessons well, for an educated man can make a better soldier, a better ditcher, or well digger, and a more perfect gentleman than an uneducated one.

Your brother, truly,
JOHN C. WEST.

LETTER No. VII.
CHAMBERSBURG, PA, JUNE 29, 1863

MY PRECIOUS WIFE:

I had not intended to write until the 9th of July, or until a battle occurred, but the reception of your most welcome letter on yesterday, of date May 11th and 13th, together with the fact that I have a prospect of a day's rest, have made me conclude to try the experiment of sending a few lines from the enemy's country, 200 miles from Richmond. If I were certain this would reach you I could make it very interesting to you, for I have endured and passed through a great deal which no one can dream of, or picture, except those who have passed through the same trials.

Newspaper writers and correspondents cannot convey any idea of the hardships of a soldier's life when on a march. I wrote to your sister, Decca, from Millwood, twenty miles west of Harper's Ferry, and gave her quite a succinct account of my trials and marches for ten or twelve days previous, and since that time I have had a repetition of the same. I have told her to write to you every two or three weeks, and have written to Miss Nannie Norton, making the same request of her, so that if you do not hear from me, or one of them, you must take it for granted that the letters do not get through the lines, and not think that anything is wrong with me, for I will be preserved safe from all harm. Nothing but a special providence could have saved me in perfect health and strength thus far.

We have marched in heat until stalwart men, apparently much stronger than myself, have fallen dead by the roadside. We have crossed and re-crossed streams, waist deep, with water cold and chilling. We have passed four or five nights and days without changing clothes, which were soaking wet during the entire time. Billy Dunklin, Billy Robinson and myself slept one night together on the very top of the Blue Ridge Mountains under a single blanket. It rained and blew furiously during the whole night, and we got up in the morning with our feet and hands shriveled just as you frequently see from remaining too long in the water. On several occasions we have waded streams just at sundown and slept in wet clothes, or sit up naked while our clothes were drying, with a prospect of being ordered to march between midnight and day. A soldier's motto is to sleep at all hazards whenever he has a chance, for it never comes amiss. We crossed the Potomac, at Williamsport, on the 26th of June, and have since marched through Greencastle and on to this place, passing through the most beautiful country I ever beheld, increasing in its charms ever since we left Culpepper. We are now between the Blue Ridge and the Allegheny; the entire landscape covered with the most magnificent farms, orchards and gardens, for miles along the road. The most neat and elegant residences and barns; positively more tastily built than two-thirds of the houses in Waco, and as fine as the dwelling houses anywhere. I have not seen a barn in the last three days that was not more substantially and carefully built and fitted out than any house I have ever seen in the country in Texas.

Wheat is the staple product in this portion of Pennsylvania, and the crops are splendid; just ready to cut. The apple trees are loaded and the cherries delicious. I enclose two varieties of cherry seed, and will endeavor to bring some if I ever get back. The people here have quite a chagrined and subdued look as we march through these towns and villages. A lady encouraged some little girls to sing the "Red, White and Blue" as we passed through Chambersburg. She remarked as I passed, "Thank God, you will never come back alive." I replied, "No, as we intend to go to Cincinnati by way of New York."

My impression is that we will have a desperate battle in a few days; but I cannot tell, as a soldier who minds is own business knows less than an outsider. I would not have missed this campaign for $500.00. I believe that if successful it will do a great deal towards bringing about a peace or our recognition by foreign powers. All of our company are doing well. Allen Killingsworth is below Richmond on a furlough. Burwell Aycock is nursing his wounds at Chattanooga. Jim Manahan is quite sick today, and has not been well for several days. I think he had a sunstroke on one of those fearfully hot days. John Harrington has not been with the company for three months. He is at Richmond. The rest are all well, Selman, Mullins et al. I am rejoiced at your progress in Latin, and in your music, and think that if anything could make me love you more, or cause us to live more happily together, if possible, it will be the consciousness of having the most accomplished wife, as well as the most charming in other respects, in the whole country. I am glad the little boys are with you, and trust they will give you no trouble. It strengthens and encourages me to know that you are cultivating and improving yourself, instead of sitting down listlessly, dipping snuff "for company," or gossiping idly. Guard against the last especially. Tell Stark and Mary not to forget their lessons, or me, and that I will come back some of these days and hear them. You ought to have no difficulty about the war tax. If the tax collector is a man of sense he can give you all the assistance you require, except the money to pay the tax. As far as my salary is concerned, you will have nothing to do with that. You had better send Dr. Combs his money as soon as you can spare, it. I have paid all the debts I contracted on the way here except $75.00

65

to Major Holman. I have $50.00 bounty and $30.00 pay
due me in the course of a week, and as there may be
a battle soon I will not draw it, but will leave it in the
hands of somebody so that you can get it, as I do not
wish a Yankee to make anything by rifling my pockets
on the battlefield. I intended to finish this sheet but it
has commenced to rain and I must bid you goodbye and
get under my blanket. May God preserve you and our
little darlings until we meet again—be it soon or late.
Love to our friends.

Your husband, faithfully ever,

JOHN C. WEST.

LETTER No. VIII.
HAGERSTOWN, MD, JULY 8, 1863
To Master Stark West, four years old.

MY DEAR LITTLE MAN:

I wrote to mamma from our camp near Chambersburg, Pennsylvania, and as tomorrow is your birthday,
and you are getting to be a big boy, I thought you would
like for papa to write you a letter and tell you something
about the war and the poor soldiers.

God has been very good to me since I wrote to mamma. He has saved my life when many thousands of good
men have been slain all around me. On the 1st, 2nd and
3rd of July a very terrible battle was fought near Gettysburg. We marched all night, leaving camp at 2 o'clock in
the afternoon in order to reach the battlefield in time.
There had been some fighting on the 1st and we passed
a hospital where I saw a great many wounded soldiers,
who were mangled and bruised in every possible way,
some with their eyes shot out, some with their arms, or
hands, or fingers, or feet or legs shot off, and all seeming

to suffer a great deal. About two miles farther on I found a great many soldiers drawn up in a line, ready to meet the Yankees, who formed another line a mile or two in front of them. These lines were three or four miles long, and at different places on the hills were the batteries of artillery.

These, you know, are cannons, which shoot large shells, and iron balls a long distance. We kept in this line so long, and I was so tired, I went to sleep and dreamed about you and mamma and little sister, and I asked God to take care of you if I am taken away from you. After awhile we were marched off in a great hurry towards the left of the Yankee line of battle, which is called the left wing, and was opposite to our right wing, which was composed principally of Hood's division. Our brigade was ordered to charge upon one of the Yankee batteries, which was posted on a mountain as high as Mount Bonnell, with another battery on a still higher mountain, just back of it, to support it. We were standing in an open field, under the shot and shell of these batteries, for half an hour, before we moved forward, and a good many soldiers were killed all around me. One poor fellow had his head knocked off in a few feet of me, and I felt all the time as if I would never see you and little sister again. When the command was given to charge we moved forward as fast as we could towards the battery. It was between a half and three-quarters of a mile across an open field, over a marshy branch, over a stone fence, and up a very rugged and rocky hill, while Yankee sharpshooters were on the higher mountains, so as to have fairer shots at our officers. On we went yelling and whooping, and soon drove the Yankees from the first battery, but were too much worn out and exhausted to climb to the second, besides a great many of our men were killed, and minnie bullets and grape shot were as thick as hail, and we were compelled to get behind the rocks and trees to save ourselves.

We renewed the charge several times, but the slaughter of our men was so great that after four or five efforts to advance we retired about sunset and slept behind the rocks. I had thrown away my blanket and everything except my musket and cartridge box in the fight, and so spent a very uncomfortable night. We remained at the same place all the next day, and every now and then Yankee bullets would come pretty thick amongst us. One bullet went through my beard and struck a rock half an inch from my head, and a piece of the bullet hit me on the lip and brought the blood. Lieutenant Joe Smith, of McLennan County, was killed in ten feet of me, and John Terry and Tom Mullens were both wounded in the shoulders. I wanted to write my little man a letter, which he could read when he was a big boy, but it has been raining and the ground is very wet and everything so uncomfortable that I cannot enjoy it.

Tell mamma she had better put off her visit to South Carolina until the war is over, as she seems to be doing very well, and it will be better for her.

Your father, truly,
JOHN C. WEST

LETTER No. IX.
CAMP NEAR HAGERSTOWN, MD, JULY 9, 1863

MY PRECIOUS WIFE:

On yesterday I wrote a bungling letter to my "little man" intending it for his birthday, as I feared we would be ordered off today, and sure enough I have just learned we are to leave directly. God has mercifully preserved me through the terrible battle of Gettysburg, though my escape was as narrow as possible. I cannot attempt an account of the battle as a private only knows what occurred in his immediate presence. Our regiment went into the fight with 350 and lost 150 in killed, wounded and missing. Lieutenant Joe Smith, son of Captain Jack Smith, on Hog Creek, was killed. We had just climbed a stone fence and crossed a branch and little marsh. Lieutenant Smith had wet his handkerchief in the branch and tied it around his head. It was extremely hot. It was about 3 o'clock in the afternoon, and we had double-quicked across an open field for nearly 500 yards. He was killed in twenty feet of me, just after we crossed the branch—shot through the head, the bullet passing through the folds of his handkerchief on both sides. He was a splendid officer and we miss him very much.

From the 1st to the 6th of July I never took off my accouterments night or day. I marked in my Bible the Psalm which I read while in the line of battle among the rocks on the third of July. We were somewhat in advance of our main line and held our place, but could drive the enemy no further neither could they dislodge us. We remained there until the close of the battle. I have requested my friends to save my Bible and the little tin cup, which baby gave me for you in case of my fall. I threw away my blankets and all of my extra clothing when we went into the battle, but I picked up a blanket on coming out. You need not trouble yourself about my wants, as it is impossible to make a soldier comfortable. I was soaking wet from the 2nd to the 6th of July, without meat and with little bread, and have been for some time; so you see if I had all the comforts you might fix for me, I would have to throw them away on a long, wet march. It is impossible to carry them. I started from Texas to find a fight, and I have made a success of it. I am much delighted and gratified at the way in which you seem to be spending your time. With kisses for the little ones, I am,

Your husband, faithfully ever,
JOHN C. WEST

LETTER No. X.
CAMP NEAR CULPEPPER, C. H., JULY 27, 1863

Major Charles S. West, Judge Advocate
General of Trans-Mississippi Department.

DEAR BROTHER:

I would have attempted a letter to you long ago, but the difficulties presented to a private on a regular march unfit him for anything like recreation, and the uncertainty of getting a letter across the Mississippi disinclined me to make the attempt amid the confusion of camp life. If I were seated in a comfortable chair instead of having my naked buttocks upon the sand (for my last article of underwear is in the wash and the seat of my pants is in Pennsylvania,) I could give you a succinct account of the campaign into the enemy's country; whereas you must be satisfied with this hurried and meager history which Captain W. H. Hammon, our quartermaster, has promised me to mail across the river. We left the camp from which I now write on the fifteenth day of June, under a burning sun and a brazen sky. The march was conducted by that unmerciful driver, our beloved General Hood, who simply strikes a trot and is satisfied that the Texas Brigade at least will camp with him at nightfall. We moved twenty-four miles on that day, camping near Gaines' Cross Roads, with the loss of two hundred men from sunstroke.

The road for the last ten miles was literally lined with soldiers fallen from exhaustion. We were required to wade Hazel run, two branches of the Rappahanock, the Shenandoah and other minor streams, under positive orders not to stop to pull off or roll up. We crossed the last named on the afternoon of the 18th, and camped about a mile from it.

On the 19th we marched down the river and recrossed at Snigger's Gap on the summit of the Blue Ridge. At those last two camps we were drenched in the hardest rains I ever saw, pouring down during the entire night. On the 20th, in the morning, we built a rock fence half a mile long and made all necessary arrangements to defend the Gap if required. On the afternoon of the same day we re-crossed the river and camped on the north side, four miles from Berryville. On the 21st marched ten miles down the river and three miles out from it through Millwood, and camped two miles from it and within four miles of Berryville on the regular turnpike, which passes through Martinsburg, Smithfield and several other smaller places.

At this camp it was formally announced that "we are about to go into the enemy's country, that private property should be respected, that all pillaging and private foraging and should be abstained from as the troops would be subsisted upon the very best the enemy's country afforded." This amounted to an official falsehood or mistake, as the sequel showed. We trudged on, nothing occurring worthy of record until the twenty-sixth, on which we took breakfast in Virginia, dragged through mud and rain to the Potomac, crossed it at Williamsport, and were halted two miles beyond with the promise of rations and of time to cook them. Our wood was gathered, fires kindled, a stiff drink of whiskey issued to each man (about one-third got pretty tight), and the order to march was given. We dragged—many slipped, down and literally rolled over in the mud (for it rained

71

all the time), and among the most conspicuous was Captain M. of the ** Texas, one of your legislative brethren; and finally, about dusk we reached the Pennsylvania line and took supper in the United States. A brilliant and eventful day! Breakfast in Virginia, whiskey in Maryland and supper in Pennsylvania. The portions of the two last mentioned states through which we passed are the most thoroughly improved which I ever saw. There was not a foot of surplus or waste territory. All had been made to answer the demands of the consumer. Wheat, corn, clover, half a dozen varieties of grass, rye, barley—all in full growth and approaching maturity—met the eye at every turn, all enclosed in rock or strongly and closely built wooden fences. Apples, cherries, currants, pears, quinces, etc, in the utmost profusion, and bee hives ad infinitum. The barns were, however, the most striking feature of the landscape, for it was one bright panorama for miles. They invariably occupied the most select building site on the tract, and were equal in size, elegance and finish, and superior in arrangement and adaptation to this purpose to three-fourths of the dwellings in Texas. On the other hand, the dwellings, though neat and comfortable, were secreted in some nook or corner, as if there had been a close calculation that a horse or an ox being the larger animal, required a more spacious residence than a human being. I think the class or position in society must depend somewhat on the size and elegance of the barn.

The springs and milk houses or dairies were also a noted feature of the country. I think I have seen more than fifty springs equal to those of Barton, San Antonio, San Marcos and Salado.

But the most singular phenomenon which impressed me was the scarcity of visible inhabitants, in this apparently densely populated region. Women and children were seen peeping about but as shy as partridges, but in the towns and villages men, women and children thronged by hundreds. I believe two brigades of able-bodied men under thirty years of age could have been raised in Chambersburg alone. We were, of course, coldly received everywhere.

Our camp was not more than two miles beyond Chambersburg on the night of June 27. On the 29th we moved ten or twelve miles to Fayetteville and were encamped there until the evening of the 1st of July, the day on which the fight at Gettysburg was opened. About dusk we started for the battlefield, Hill and Ewell having driven the enemy four miles back on that day. General Lee, it was said among the men, was opposed to giving battle at that point, and in favor of giving the enemy the slip (I don't know how), and marching straight for Baltimore. It was found that this would be impracticable, owing to the difficulty of protecting twenty or twenty-five miles of train from Yankee cavalry. It was then suggested to burn one-half the train. It was opposed by the argument that the subsistence would not be sufficient and the consequent risk of demoralization for want of food. General Lee then said to fight was the only chance, and he was fully satisfied of a complete victory.

Generals Longstreet and Hood were opposed to attacking the enemy in a position of their own choosing. I am unable without a map to describe the locality of the forces or the face of the country along the entire line, but can give you a faint idea of affairs on the right wing. Hood's division occupied this, and our brigade was the last but one on the extreme right of the division. The line must have been five or six miles long. We were put into the fight about 3 o'clock in the afternoon of the 2nd, having marched all night on the 1st and laid in line of battle all the morning of the 2nd, and my first lesson as a recruit was to lie for about half an hour under what the most experienced soldiers called the worst shelling they ever witnessed. Several were killed and many wounded in a few feet of me, and the infernal machines came tearing and whirring through the ranks with a most demoralizing tendency. This, however, was soon over. Our line was formed, and with a voice that Stentor might have envied, General Hood gave the command: "Forward—steady!—Forward!" (He was on horseback, on the left of a line from our brigade to the battery playing upon us, and about three hundred yards from me.) And forward we went. The word was passed down the line, "Quick, but not double quick," but we moved as fast as we could. Off went blankets, knapsacks and all surplus baggage, and yelling and screaming we rushed on the batteries—one on a lofty eminence beyond a rock fence and a small branch, the other back of it on quite a mountain about three hundred yards farther off and a little to the right—were full three-quarters of a mile from us when the word "forward" was given. The result was the line became broken and confused and the men exhausted (having marched all of the previous night) by the time they reached the foot of the hill. Nevertheless, the first battery was taken, and after rallying in the best manner possible, several desperate efforts were made to charge the second, but courage and even desperation was useless. There were places full ten or fifteen feet perpendicular around which we were compelled to go, and the entire ascent would have been difficult to a man entirely divested of gun and accouterments. It was a mass of rock and boulders amid which a mountain goat would have reveled, and being subjected to a fire on our left flank, made it a most dangerous and unsafe place for a soldier, and many a fellow reminded me of the alliteration, "Round the rude rock the ragged rascal ran."

Our assault, with short intervals, was kept up until dark, when we rested on our arms and spent an uneasy night amid the crags. Our position was now rather in advance of the troops on our left. All day on the 3rd we held our ground, making unsuccessful sallies, checking skirmishers and passing shots with sharpshooters, one of whom, secreted in a tree on the side of the mountain, put a bullet within an inch of my head as I leaned against a rock, part of the bullet flying into my lip.

About 4 o'clock in the afternoon cannonading was opened along the entire line, and such a thundering and crashing and roaring surely was never heard. An eagle in the very midst of a tremendous thunderstorm might possibly have experienced such confusion. All agreed that Sharpsburg and Second Mannassas was not a priming to it. Milton's account of the great battle between the combined forces of good and evil, which originated in this same question of secession, gives some faint idea of this artillery duel.

Later in the afternoon we heard terrible musketry on our left and yells and huzzahs swaying alternately back and forth as the line gave way, first one side and then the other. We could not see through the timber, but the location of the final huzzahs satisfied us that our center was giving way. This compelled us to withdraw down the mountain and out in the open field to prevent being flanked, which we accomplished with the loss of a few men. The fighting here ceased, darkness preventing either party from making any important move. We threw up breastworks on the 4th, with the hope that the enemy would leave his position in the mountains and attack us on the open plain, where we could have routed him and kept him in such confusion that a rally would have been impossible.

I believe the wounding of General Hood early in the

75

action was the greatest misfortune of the day. Our position could have been held by very few men, and if a considerable force had been thrown around the mountain to our right the enemy would have been routed in half an hour. I think many of the Federal army would have deserted, being in easy reach of home. Baltimore would have been ours and the New York riots would have been as famous as the battle of Bunker Hill.

As it is, let who will say to the contrary, we made Mannassas time from Pennsylvania. It is unnecessary to give any detailed account of myself. Suffice it to say I have endured more than I believed myself capable of. I have been through a campaign and participated in a furious and terrible battle. I am satisfied that I am not afraid to go into another, though, since the fall of Vicksburg, I prefer to be west of the Mississippi, closer to Texas and closer to my family. I would like to have a long talk with you, and hope for the better days when we can enjoy it. Write to my wife and let her know that you have received this letter. I had intended to allude to that "official falsehood" referred to above, but let it pass. Suffice it to say that if we had depended on our commissaries, we would have suffered seriously for food.

Your brother, truly,

JOHN C. WEST

LETTER No. XI.
CAMP NEAR CULPEPPER, JULY 28, 1863

MY PRECIOUS WIFE:

I wrote you quite a full letter yesterday and sent it to the Fourth Texas Department at Richmond, the agent for which is very particular in seeking opportunities to send letters across the river, but still it may not reach you, so I have determined to try another channel which I have found today. Captain Hammon, quartermaster of our regiment will start for Texas tomorrow and has kindly consented to take this for me. You see by the caption that I am back at our old camp, which I am beginning to regard as home. I am sitting near the same spot from which I wrote you more than a month ago, and my surroundings pretty much the same, except the absence of our Lieutenant, Joe Smith, who was killed at Gettysburg.

He was a very talented and excellent officer, enjoying, perhaps, more than any officer in the regiment, the confidence and trust of headquarters. His loss is a very serious blow to the company.

By the goodness of God I came safely through, though many were killed around me. One bullet passed through my beard, grazed my ear and struck a rock about an inch from my head. A piece of the lead flew into my upper lip, but caused no interruption or serious inconvenience. Our move into Pennsylvania was a failure, and I think General Lee never would have attacked the enemy in their position on the mountainside except for the splendid condition of his army, and his confidence in its ability to accomplish anything he chose to attempt. Our division was on the right of the entire line and our brigade the last but one on the extreme right of the division, and just opposite to one of the strongest positions of the enemy, which was on a high mountain and defended by batteries on mountains still higher. We took and held the lower heights long enough to capture the batteries, but were unable after several charges to scale the higher ones, being subjected to a fire on our left flank and in front while attempting to climb over rocks and gorges, which would have delighted a mountain goat.

On the third day, late in the evening, our center gave

way, and we were compelled to retire down the mountain and take our position in the open field, where we threw up breastworks and awaited the advance of the enemy. We remained here during the entire fourth day of July, and such another fourth I never expect to spend. We had no meat and very little bread for two days. Had not taken off our accouterments during the time, and the rain poured incessantly, so that the water on the level plain was two or three inches deep. On the following evening we discovered that the enemy were satisfied and were moving off. We were in no condition to follow. We remained on the battlefield until 2 o'clock at night, during which time I snatched a nap or two by lying on three rails, which kept me above water. In the battle I threw away my haversack and contents, except a flannel shirt and a pair of socks, which I tucked under my belt. I lost the socks and have been for several days without any, but have not experienced the inconvenience I expected, except in having my ankles considerably lacerated by briers in marching across the fields. I have had no change of clothing since, and hence have been compelled to throw away my undershirt, which had become a harbor for innumerable body lice. Don't blush or be shocked; no true soldier is free from them, and I will scrub well before I come home. I am having my only underwear washed today, and owing to a large rent in my pants, would be subject to arrest in any well managed city, for improper exposure of my person in a public place. However, these are small matters, and we will smile over them in the better days to come. You must not try to send me anything, or trouble yourself in the least degree about me, unless you choose to send me some little token by someone who will deliver it to the agent of the Fourth Texas Department at Richmond. I have left you to take care of yourself, and you must not be disturbed about me. God will take charge of both of us. I have experienced no inconvenience in health for want of clothing. Since I have been here Allen Killingsworth has given me a pair of socks, and while I write this sentence Charley Darby sends me another pair; so I have two pair, and feel flush on socks. I have a good pair of pants in Richmond, and another for winter in Columbia, so don't trouble yourself by thinking of me or my misfortunes, but smile, chat and keep well. Attend to your music, your Latin and the improvement of the children. Watch your chickens and turkeys as if you expected me home to eat them as soon as they are grown. I wrote to you and Stark on the 8th and 9th from Hagerstown, and this is the second letter since then.

I have no idea that you will ever get the others, but some hope that this will reach you. All the Waco boys are well and at their posts now, except Herrington, Clark and Majors. Herrington is in the hospital on account of his eyes, Majors is on the way to us now and Clark is at Sulphur Springs. Since Vicksburg has fallen I think you had better not attempt to go to South Carolina. You are safer in Texas. Our cause looks a little gloomy now, but I have no fears of the final result. I believe the war has been prolonged by the late success of the enemy, and perhaps it would be better if I were on your side of the Mississippi. I said in my letter yesterday that we would have another great battle in twenty days, but I hear now that it is the opinion of our generals that there will be no considerable engagement for several weeks, though nothing is certain.

I wrote to the attorney-general of the Confederacy yesterday that I had left my office in Texas and gone into the army, and saying that I would return to Texas if he thought it desirable or necessary, but I believe I am where I ought to be and I think he will sanction my course. Every able-bodied man ought to be where he can strike the hardest blow for his country.

I received a letter from Decca Stark of June 23rd. Lamar, Douglass and sister Mac are in Columbia. I doubt not we will have a reunion after awhile. You and the friends whom I have named must still offer your prayers for me, and I shall fear no harm, for nothing but the special favor of God has preserved me thus far. Tell Stark and Mary to obey you and get their lessons, and when I come home I will take one on each knee and tell them about the soldiers. Remember me to the servants. May God and the good angels guard you and the little darlings. I have had but one letter from you.

Your husband, faithfully ever,
John C. West

LETTER No. XII.
Camp Near Fredericksburg, Va., August 7, 1863

My Precious Wife:

We have just heard of the death of Colonel B. H. Carter. He was wounded at Gettysburg—twice in the leg, and in the face, and left in the hands of the enemy. I wrote you not more than a week ago quite a long letter by Captain Hammon, telling you all about my Pennsylvania trip, a full narrative of which could be made quite readable, but I am not conveniently situated for thinking or writing, so as to render the undertaking feasible. I am having a pretty hard time of it, but heaven is blessing me continually with good health, and I believe will save me to the end.

You must not be uneasy about me when you do not hear from me. I have received but one letter from you since I left home, yet I am satisfied that all is well, and, strange to say, I have no desire to return home while the war lasts. I believe this disposition has been especially vouchsafed me in order that I may b fully prepared for all the hardships that befall me. Since the fall of Vicksburg I have not had much hope of hearing from you, though, to our surprise, yesterday, Coella and Macon Mullens received letters of the 5th and 6th of July. This has encouraged me to hope for one from you. I have written you a great many letters from different points. You must not be uneasy if you hear of me being destitute or in need of anything. A soldier cannot carry enough with him on a march to make him comfortable. Another hope and desire you must give up; it is almost impracticable and hopeless to attempt to recover the body of a private soldier killed in battle, so don't think about this; I can rest one place as well as another. All the Waco boys are writing today, as notice has been given that a Mr. Parsons will take them to Texas. Do all you can to keep your mind employed and your face in smiles. All will yet be well for us. Pray for me, and if I am taken from you, it will be all right. I trust in God. Kisses for the children.

Your husband, faithfully ever,

JOHN C. WEST

LETTER No. XIII.
CAMP NEAR FREDERICKSBURG, AUGUST 14, 1863

To Mrs. Theodore Stark, Columbia, South Carolina.

DEAR MOTHER:

Yesterday was quite an exciting time among the soldiers. We were paid off our dues up to July 1st, and everybody consequently felt very rich. A great many bet at cards, who would never do so at home, because they have nothing else to do. It is a sort of frolic and pastime, and a good many have already lost all they had. My pay amounted to $79.70. I enclose $50 of it in this letter, which you will please keep for me, as I may get sick, or wounded someday, and need it,and can then borrow with a clear conscience, knowing I have the wherewith to pay. I will retain the balance to buy peas, rice, dried apples, etc., which our butler has. You can keep the money for Mary, or use it for her benefit, in case I should ever be missing at the fireside. I trust the report of General Hood's promotion to Lieutenant-Colonel of cavalry is true, and also of General Hampton to Major-General. I think Hood would endeavor to mount our brigade. Love to all.

Your son, truly,
JOHN C. WEST

LETTER No. XIV.
CAMP NEAR FREDERICKSBURG, AUGUST 17, 1863

MY PRECIOUS WIFE:

I have just learned that Colonel Sweet, of San Antonio, will start across the Mississippi in a day or two. I have no chance to write a letter. It is 9 o'clock at night; I am writing by a campfire with twenty men talking all around me. No news. I am stronger and in better health than I ever was in my life. Joe Ben Majors and Burwell Aycock reached us yesterday, and several others from the hospital. I wrote to Sister Mary Blair yesterday without knowing there would be an opportunity of sending it.

All the Waco boys are well. Love to Mr. and Mrs. Carter and Bro. Burleson, etc. Kiss the litle darlings for me.

Your husband, faithfully ever,
JOHN C. WEST

LETTER No. XV.
WILMINGTON, NORTH CAROLINA, SEPTEMBER 11, 1863

MY PRECIOUS WIFE:

I am at this place on my way to Bragg's army. Our division has been ordered there. Of course in a hurried letter I can give you no account of the movements of our armies. Suffice it to say that we are not whipped on this side of the river yet, and I do not believe the combined Yankee army can subjugate the Texas brigade, though they may all be killed. I have met Major Hampton Gibbs here, and have spent most of the day with him visiting the blockaders, and he has extended to me every courtesy possible, and I shall recollect my detention in Wilmington with pleasure. I have had but one letter from you since I left Texas, but feel satisfied that all is well.

Brother Charles wrote to me in August and said you were all well up to the 10th of July. Douglas De Saussure was wounded in the shoulder a few days ago at Charleston, so I expect to see him in passing through Columbia, as I have permission to go by there. This will be sent by blockader *Elizabeth*. Hampton Gibbs sends regards to you.

Your husband, faithfully ever,
JOHN C. WEST

LETTER No. XVI
BY CAMPFIRE, 2½ MILES FROM CHATTANOOGA,
SEPTEMBER 24, 1863

MY PRECIOUS WIFE:

God has heard your prayers, and through His mercy I am preserved through the perils of another great battle, far more dangerous in its individual and personal incidents to our brigade than any of the war. The oldest soldiers agree that they have never seen the like. The line of battle was only about two and a half miles long, and we advanced upon each other in column after column, one pushing on as another fell back. We were in open woods (neither party having any breastworks worthy the name), and coming up face to face, bayonet to bayonet. Our company got into a very hot place. The musketry was almost continuous from early morning till late in the evening for two days. It occurred about ten miles from Chattanooga, in the northwest corner of Georgia, on the Chickamauga river. Our casualties (Company E) as follows: Captain Joe Billingsly, Lieutenant Allen Killingsworth, privates ___ Miller, Tom Norwood, ____ Hicks, and Whitehead, killed; Sam Chambers and Durham Holloway, severely wounded and missing; Boze Chapman, J. W. Pamplin, Billy Burton and Fred Makeig, wounded, respectively in the thigh, hand, arm and neck. I got mixed up with the Yanks by being too fast. I have the credit of doing some good work at close quarters. When their line was broken, I took my bayonet off my musket because it hurt my hand in loading rapidly, and just as I put it in the scabbard one fellow took a fair shot at me in an open place about thirty steps off. The bullet hit the handle of my bayonet, which had not been in my belt two seconds, and knocked the handle entirely off. It was driven against me with great force, blinding and sickening me so that I fell and was supposed to be fatally wounded. It seems to me that a thousand bullets and grapeshot tore up the ground around me. As soon as I was able I crawled to a tree and afterwards to the rear, to the field hospital in a barnyard, where I remained all night. I was pretty sore but able to march, so I went back to the line of battle early next morning. I thought of Waco and its peaceful days and the sweet-faced, innocent children on their way to church.

Our brigade went in again about 3 o'clock in the afternoon, and I received a lick from something, I do not know what, on the wrist, which was very painful for a day or two, but when we found that the Yankees were gone and the field was ours, I was much rejoiced. Many of these Yankee soldiers were Germans who could not speak English. I got, on the battlefield, a new blue-backed Webster spelling book, which I will send home to the children.

I got a splendid gun and accouterments, plenty of paper and a nice pair of woolen gloves. I cannot speak of the movements of the army, for I know nothing. I know that we are now in line of battle at the foot of Lookout Mountain and expect an attack in the morning. Our pickets had some skirmishing this afternoon, but the main body did not advance. I trust that God will spare my life, and have prayed Him to watch over you and the little ones if I am taken. You must not hope to get my body if I am killed, as it will be impossible to do otherwise than leave me on the field in a soldier's careless grave.

I stopped in Columbia two days when passing and found all well but Douglas De Saussure, who is suffering from a wound in the shoulder received at Charleston. You have some new cousins in Columbia—the Wilkinsons—refugees from New Orleans. Mrs. Wilkinson's name was Mary Stark. They are nice, sweet girls. Their father was colonel of a Louisiana regiment and was killed at Manassas.

At Chickamauga General Hood was wounded in the right leg and it has been amputated. As we were going into the fight he rode down the line in our rear towards our right he said: "Move up, men; those fellows are shooting in the tops of the trees." We thought then that he was a little too close in. The old Texas brigade is fearfully cut up. There are not more than 150 in our regiment.

The Fifth numbers about 100 and the First about the same. There is said to be a company in the First Texas with one officer and no men left; another has one man left. Our company has about twenty-five men. Of course there is exaggeration in these statements, but we are terribly thinned out. All of the men whose names I have given above as killed or wounded fell in a space of not more than sixty feet square, except Captain Billingsley, who was killed at a different place on the afternoon of the second day, as we backed out from a charge across an open field, which got too hot to stay in. As I went to the rear after being wounded, I met General Benning of Georgia. He was bare-headed and riding an artillery horse with the harness on him. He said, "Where are you going?" I showed him my wound. He said, "Great God! is everybody killed? I have lost my brigade." It did look in some spots as if the killed outnumbered the living.

There was a gallant Wisconsin officer killed in front of our Fourth Texas. One of the litter bearers gave me his sword, which I carried to the field hospital. It was beautifully mounted and engraved, "Captain Haup, Company E, Fifteenth Wisconsin Volunteers."

You must keep in good spirits and don't allow yourself to mope or feel uneasy. God knows best, and if I am hurt it is all right. Sometimes my faith is unwavering and I feel perfectly safe, and I have no doubt that He will watch over you and the little ones. Kiss them for me every day and go on with your Latin and music. May God and the good angels guard you.

Your husband, faithfully ever,

John C. West

LETTER No. XVII.
In Line of Battle Near Chattanooga., October 13, 1863

Major Charles S. West, Judge Advocate
General of Trans-Mississippi Department.

Dear Brother:

Three weeks have passed since the battle of Chickamauga, and I have not until now had an opportunity of writing to you as I had intended, immediately after the fight.

Our brigade left Port Royal, Va., on the 8th of September and came by rail to a burnt bridge, near Ringgold, in northeast Georgia. I had permission to stop in Columbia, S. C., where I spent two days very agreeably, using the opportunity to have my clothing washed, and to get rid of vermin, which skirmish at will over the soldier's body. The old brigade fell in love with South Carolina's hospitality.

At every depot and station throughout the state the ladies, old and young, flocked in loaded with baskets of provisions, fruits and delicacies of every character which these scant times afford, which were offered amid smiles and tears and expressions of congratulations and encouragement to every soldier. Rags and dirt seemed to be a recommendation where gilt and brass failed to excite attention. It is useless to enter into incidents; suffice it to say that the reception all through the state was all that the speed and confusion would allow. I overtook the brigade on the morning of September 18th, at the burnt bridge just at the dawn of day and found all astir and making ready to move. I had no time to rest, but marched off immediately, passing Ringgold between eight and nine o'clock in the morning. Here we first heard of Yanks ahead, and putting out flankers moved on cautiously and slowly. At about twelve o'clock, while

passing through quite a narrow defile, we heard considerable firing in front. We were ordered to load and await
orders. While here I saw citizens, men, women and children making the best of their time in getting to the rear.
One poor woman was overloaded with coverlets, tin pans
and other utensils, with a child on each side and two or
three bawling behind. She fell down two or three times,
but scrambled on for life while muskets sputtered in the
surrounding hills. I could not help thinking of "woe unto
those who are with child and who give suck in those
days." We soon moved off the road by the left flank and
were drawn up and advanced in line of battle for about
half mile and halted. We remained here awaiting devel-
opments, while cavalry were dashing hither and thither,
feeling the pulse of the enemy and discovering his positions. We now crossed the Chickamauga at Lee's mill
and moved on about two miles and were again formed in
line of battle and advanced about half a mile across some
very pretty little fields, with hills on the opposite side,
suggesting the idea of sharpshooters, &c.; indeed, we all
expected a volley every moment and went through all
the fears and motions incident to entering a charge. We
were much relieved at finding only some cavalry who
discharged a few shots too high to hit anybody and disappeared without a shot from our side. Here we remained
in line of battle until nearly dark, when we moved on
and camped about eight o'clock. Judging by the moving
of troops and the rumbling of artillery during the night,
I felt pretty sure that "the wool-tearing"would come off
in the morning. We remained at our camp (occasional
firing being heard on our right) where our line of battle
was being formed, until about ten o'clock, when we proceeded about a mile and a half, being about ten miles
from Chattanooga, and took our place in the line near
the center. About half past ten or eleven o'clock a most

tremendous fire of musketry was opened on our right, which continued for two hours without two minutes intermission. The country from this point to Chattanooga is an undulating pine and oak region, as you find in upper portions of South Carolina and Georgia—such as we roamed over about Camden in our boyhood days. So there was no trouble for anybody to get into the fight who was willing and anxious, no excuse for skulking or straggling. It was simply to move forward and whip the enemy in pretty open ground or be whipped back again.

There were no breastworks worth the name. The line of battle seemed to be short, not more than three miles long, and both sides had their troops in heavy masses, one behind the other. When relief was wanted it was nearly always in sight; in fact, you could look back and see your support waiting their turn to "go in." This accounts for the unceasing fire of musketry. The locality was not well adapted generally to the use of artillery, but grape and cannister did some good work in the open fields.

Deducting the intervals necessary for reforming and relieving exhausted troops (and these intervals were very short), there must have been eight hours of un-intermitted musketry on each day. It reminded me of rain on a tin roof, where at intervals the storm rages with tremendous fury, then lulls but still continues as sounds grow faint or distinct according to the changes of the varying wind. Our turn came about 4 o'clock in the afternoon. We advanced to within one hundred yards of the Yanks, when I could see them plainly lying and squatting in the bushes and scant undergrowth. There was a small field beyond them and a little hill on the other side of it, from which a battery annoyed us a little as we advanced, but had no serious effect on our progress. Just as I saw the Yanks and was about to shoot, a

cry passed up the line that these were our own men, but
very few seemed to regard it, and a pretty steady fire
was opened on them and promptly returned. I had fired
five or six shots, not over thirty steps, when the whole
line in front of us seemed broken and confused, except
two or three companies behind a cabin on my left. I was
too much excited to notice any except those fleeing in
my front. I rushed on, waving my hat, until I was pretty
well mixed up with them and was knocked down, and
fell almost upon the body of a severely wounded Yank,
who asked me to unbuckle his belt, which I did with
great difficulty, for I was very sick and spitting blood
myself. He died before he had time to thank me. A ball
had struck the handle of my bayonet, driving it against
me, knocking it to pieces, and glancing downward,
passed through my clothing, coming out about my right
hip. I laid here some minutes, with minnies and grape
showering about me and knocking the dirt over me. I got
to the rear by a miracle. I went to the field hospital and
remained until morning and then returned to the company about daylight, bruised and pretty sore but able to
shoot. We fought over the same kind of ground the next
day, driving the Yanks back all the time. Our brigade
pushed them about a half a mile about 1 o'clock p. m.,
and I believe would have captured a great many but for
a flank fire by mistake from our own men. I was hit on
my right wrist, making a bruise which hurt me for several days.

On Monday morning the Yanks were gone. I could hear
artillery, which I presume was hurrying up their retreat.
It is said among the men here that General Bragg has
put Generals Polk, Hindman and Forrest under arrest,
for what cause I do not know, but my impression is, that
with either Hood or Longstreet or Lee in command, half
of Rosecran's army would have been captured. I have

seen Bragg, Buckner, Longstreet, Breckenridge, Lee, Hood and President Davis. The three last look like great men, and would have been great in any age. I do not admire Bragg. Buckner has a fine, benevolent face. Longstreet is a bulldog soldier and cares nothing about flank movements. He makes a dead set at the center, and can whip any army on earth if he has men enough to fight until he is tired of it. Breckenridge is a game-looking, handsome man, six feet high.

We are now lying two and a half or three miles from Chattanooga, with our left resting on Lookout Mountain and our right on the river, six or seven miles from here, the line crossing Missionary Ridge, which, as Lookout Mountain, also commands a complete view of the Yankee camp. I do not understand what Rosecrans is to do. If he advances he will be whipped. He has a terrible road for sixty miles to retreat over, and has to haul his provisions over the same road if he remains in Chattanooga, with the chances of having his trains destroyed by cavalry— "Mr. Forest's critter company," as the old woman called it. She said: "They formed a line of fight right across my garden and calf lot, tore down every scrap of fence and run right over my ash-hopper, and the Lord have mussy! Goodness gracious! What a dust they did kick up!"

Our picket lines are within one hundred yards of each other, and keep up a pretty constant chat and exchange of papers, though contrary to strict orders. I see no difference between this army and the Yanks we met in Virginia. President Davis paid us a visit on the 10th of this month and rode down our entire line. He was dressed in a dark suit mixed with steel gray.

Love to your wife and all the rest.

Your brother,
JOHN C. WEST

LETTER No. XVIII.
CAMP NEAR CHATTANOOGA., OCTOBER 9, 1863

TO LITTLE STARK AND MARY WEST:

I have a nice little piece of paper which I took from a Yankee portfolio on the battlefield of Chickamauga, and thought it would be a good time to send you a little letter. You must be good children and learn to read and write, so that you can answer this letter and read to me when I come home. We have been policing our camp today, and that means to sweep and clean up just like our negroes sweep and clean the yard. The soldiers make brooms out of the brush and sweep the leaves and trash into a pile and burn it, and then we have nice clean ground to sit and to sleep on at night. We have little tents which we took from the Yankees, and they keep the frost and rain off of our heads. Every night I go to sleep with my clothes on and my hat over my face, and sometimes I stay awake nearly all night and think about you and mamma and wonder if you are all well, and if you obey and mind mamma all the time, and say your prayers. God has given you a good mamma, and you ought to love Him very much and ask Him to take care of her. God takes care of the soldiers, too, and of all good people.

The soldier who carried our flag in the last battle was killed, and Mr. Makeig took the flag and carried it until he was shot through the neck. Mr. Makeig's father lives near Waco, and you must let him know what a brave soldier his son is. He is loved by all the company and is a splendid soldier. We are very near to the Yankees now and I stand guard within sixty or one hundred yards of them, and get water out of the same creek. We talk with them and exchange newspapers, and swap tobacco for coffee. They are very tired of the war, and want to go home as badly as we do.

Your grandpa and Aunt Decca, in Columbia, got a letter from mamma and sent it to me. You must kiss mamma for me and be good children.

Your father, truly,
JOHN C. WEST.

LETTER No. XIX.
CAMP NEAR CHATTANOOGA., OCTOBER 9, 1863

MY PRECIOUS WIFE:

Your letters of 16th and 26th of July, enclosing one from Mrs. Carter, reached me three days ago, but I was sent out on picket, immediately on receiving it and had to use spade and pick all day yesterday on a redan, which prevented me from answering sooner. You cannot conceive what pleasure Mrs. Carter's letter gave me. All stereotyped newspaper paragraphs about "the poor soldier," etc., seem insipid compared to such a kind, sympathizing note from a beloved friend. I have read her letter almost as often as yours, and treasure it next to one from you. I put all the letters I brought from Texas for Georgia in the post office at Augusta with my own hand, and told Mr. Rogers at the drug store that I had done so.

Mr. Carter had gone to Charleston to attend a sale. I only saw Wiston in Richmond and asked him to attend to the delivery of the letters there as I was pressed for time.

Tell Stark that I cannot love him if he does not say his lessons and obey you and tell little blue eyes she must be smart and beat her brother reading. I am glad you were thinking of me in those hot July days, for from the 15th of June until the 27th of July was one constant march or maneuver, while we were parched with thirst, pinched with hunger, foot-sore and weary. I have written quite a full account of all these things to mother and Decca, and requested them to save the letters for you. I hope you have received all these letters, and I regret to see you so desponding about our cause. The loss of Port Hudson and Vicksburg are small affairs, and did not cause me a night's uneasiness except as cutting off communications from you, which has all the time been so doubtful that I do not consider the coming of letters as a matter of course, but only as delightful luxuries to be enjoyed "few and far between." I have had only two in six months, in which you speak of others which have never come. You must not despond about me—what if I do suffer a little—better men have died in a worse cause. I have passed through trials of endurance and of my courage to which I thought myself unequal, but the hollow of an Almighty hand has been over me, and the trials of yesterday I can smile at today. Suppose we did pass seven days and nights soaking wet, marching, eating no meat and having bread without salt?

What if we marched for days through brier fields, with worn out low-quartered shoes until our ankles were a mass of blood? What difference is it now that we frowned and groaned with pain, when the soles of our feet were one great bruise? What boots all this if we returned from the campaign stronger and in better health than we ever were before? Now, when God brings us safely through all these difficulties and saves us amid a shower of bullets, when inside the Yankee line stricken down amid the dead and wounded of the foe, exposed to a torrent of shell and grape which literally tore up the earth about us, shall we not take courage and be grateful?

We have eaten cornbread half done, made with unsifted meal, accompanied with bacon raw or broiled on a stick, for three weeks at a time—yet I am well, perfectly well. Verily I believe that God has guarded and preserved me every hour. I firmly believe that he will save me harmless through this dread day of our country's danger, or He will answer my constant prayer that I may be taken, if die I must, in the very midst of my country's foes, and that my spirit may ascend amid the smoke of battles, a fit offering to liberty and truth, and my body rest among the brave where the dead lie thickest, and here let me emphasize what I have said before, you must not cherish a hope of recovering my body if I am lost in battle. It will be the merest accident if you do so. You must not be troubled in mind continually. I can excuse some uneasiness when you hear of a battle, but do not be worried all the time. Of course there is great danger every time we go into battle. It seems to me it must be the utmost stretch of divine power to save one in the thickest of a fight. The rescue of Shadrack, Meshack and Abednego was no more a miracle than the preservation of some of us on the afternoon of Saturday, the nineteenth of September, at Chickamauga. Don't have the blues. Study your Latin, your music and your children, and leave the result to God. Kisses for the children, and love to Mrs. Carter.

Your husband, faithfully ever,

JOHN C. WEST

NOTE.—May 1, 1897. Mrs. Carter mentioned in this letter, is now Mrs. Henrietta Harrison. She is still living in Waco—in a green and beautiful old age, a joy and a benediction to a large circle of loving and devoted friends. In matters of taste and propriety her word is an oracle to the young. In works of benevolence her hand is ever ready, and the poor rise up and call her blessed. In the church her light shines more and more as toward the coming of a perfect day.

> "None know her but to love her,
> None name her but to praise."

J.C.W.

LETTER No. XX.
CAMP NEAR CHATTANOOGA., OCTOBER 20, 1863

MY PRECIOUS WIFE:

Your unusually interesting letter of August 28th, as also one of September 22nd from brother Charles, in which he said you were all well up to the tenth of September, reached me on the seventeenth of this month, and gave me great pleasure, because you seem to have been enjoying yourself, just as if you intended to use the world for all the good it can afford and I think you are right, and I trust you will take as many trips into the country as your duties at home will permit, and always try to be cheerful and happy. I like the soldiers' song that is "all the go" here now—

"Now let the wild world wag as it will,
I'll be gay and happy still," etc.

Where is the good sense in gloom and despair in anticipation of misfortune; there will be enough of life left to grieve in when trouble overtakes us, without borrowing in advance. You must not forget about the shade trees. I long to see them growing and to see the children playing under them.

We have had very disagreeable weather for two or three weeks, raining nearly all the time, but I am getting along about as usual and am perfectly well. You said nothing about the dogs, Morgan and Frank. I care very little what you do with them, as hunting is entirely out of my program now. I am sorry to hear that your meat is out, and trust that you will soon have a supply on hand. I have no doubt that your school will succeed very well, and am glad to have you try it. You must not despair of your letters reaching me. There is so much talking around me that I cannot write more at present. Love to

Mrs. Carter and other friends.

Your husband, faithfully ever,

John C. West

LETTER No. XXI.

Camp Near Chattanooga., October 24, 1863
To Mrs. Theodore Stark, Columbia, South Carolina

Mother:

Yours of the 13th inst. came to hand about three or four days ago. You are mistaken in supposing that I stint myself to send a little money home once in a while. There are so few chances of buying anything that I really have no use for money. Most of us spend money for tobacco, but I use so little that it does not amount to an item in my expenses, and when we are out of rations nothing to eat can be purchased within ten miles of us, so you see it is useless for me to keep money on hand, as I may lose it; besides I would rather it be used some time or other for Mary and the children—in case I should get beyond the reach of money.

I have a good pair of shoes now, and an extra jacket which I use as an overcoat. I have other articles of comfort for winter in my carpet-sack at Richmond, but do not know when I will have an opportunity of getting them, and a great many of our men have things deposited at the Fourth Texas depot, of which they stand much in need, and I suppose after a good many die of cold and pneumonia the authorities will take some steps to have the winter clothing brought to this place. But you need not be uneasy about me; I am getting on very well now, though not so well as for the first five months. It has been raining for the last three weeks, and I have not been thoroughly dry in that time. I forgot to tell you that I have found my Texas blanket, which someone stole from me on the cars six months ago near Kingsville, South Carolina. A man in General Mart Gary's regiment had it. I have been offered seventy-five dollars for it. You know that Gary and I were in college together. I went to his headquarters to see him, not having seen him in eight years. While talking to him I recognized my blanket spread out on some bushes to dry over a hundred yards off. The claimant seemed as much surprised to see me as I was to see the blanket. He gave a very satisfactory account of his possession, which made the history of the blanket quite interesting and strange. This blanket was woven for me in Texas out of native wool, and I prize it greatly. Love to all in Columbia.

Your son, truly,
JOHN C. WEST

LETTER No. XXII.
CAMP NEAR CHATTANOOGA., OCTOBER 31, 1863
To Mrs. James D. Blair, Austin, Texas

MY DEAR SISTER:

Your surprise of August the 6th reached me ten days ago. I call it a surprise because I thought that you trans-Mississippians were so crestfallen at the Vicksburg catastrophe as to regard yourselves as entirely cut off from friends on this side of the river, and so would cease all effort at correspondence. My wife writes me in the most gloomy and desponding strain, while my letters to her are full of hope and encouragement. The army here, that is, the Virginia army, simply looked upon the fall of Vicksburg as to be expected, and have never ceased to find opportunities to send letters home at a dollar per letter, and most of us have received as many as before, and now since the postmaster general has arranged for a regular mail, I trust you will all write me more frequently, for you have no idea what a comfort it is to stand in mud to the ankle, on an empty stomach, and read a line of comfort from sympathizers at home. Newspapers may exhaust their stereotyped phrases, and correspondents may discourse eloquently about the sufferings of the "poor soldier" until the phrase becomes a by-word and fails to excite an emotion of pity, much less a tear, but I will say now (for perhaps I may not live to say it face to face in the better day to come), that the sacrifice made and the toils endured by the *private soldier* in the service of the Confederate States cannot be appreciated or expressed in words, nor will they ever be known except to those who have shared them. Not even the officers of infantry, whose duties are almost as arduous, can tell the tale of hardships which fall to the lot of the man in the ranks. He is the lowest mud sill in this structure which is being reared, and when the edifice totters all the props and braces must be placed upon his shoulders. My thoughts are all the news I have—we seldom get a paper here. We have been in the mud for over a month in an almost continuous rain, and are not allowed to send to Richmond for blankets and overcoats, which many of us have there, because it will not be thought of until the hospitals are filled with pneumonia and pleurisy.

When some sagacious surgeon, who has been in a comfortable tent, with plenty of blankets, will suddenly discover that a barefooted man cannot well keep warm under one blanket, which has not been thoroughly dry for three weeks. I have been quite blessed. I was barefooted about a week ago, but then the water was too deep for shoes, so it made very little difference. It has never been necessary for me to take a dose of medicine yet, so you may know that I stand it pretty well, never having missed a roll call or a duty of any kind. I will write to Brother Charles in a day or two, and give him my thoughts on heroes and stragglers. The former race is not extinct, but dying out rapidly. The latter is increasing alarmingly. You observe that we have a good deal of time to think while in camp, and not on active service, and some time to read, too. I have read lately, "The Autocrat of the Breakfast Table," "Aurora Leigh," "Davenport Dunn," "Les Miserables" by Victor Hugo, and innumerable articles in magazines, which I have picked up in waste places. I now have on hand "Tasso's Jerusalem Delivered," which belongs to our quartermaster. I have carried a Bible and Milton in my knapsack all the time, so you see we are not absolutely illiterate.

Your brother, truly,
JOHN C. WEST

LETTER No. XXIII.
CAMP NEAR LOUDEN, EAST TENNESSEE, NOVEMBER 15, 1863

MY PRECIOUS WIFE:

I have been deterred from writing to you on account of our continued movement. We left the front of Chattanooga on the 5th of this month; that is, Longstreet's corps. The remainder of Bragg's army still lies in line of battle, where they have been for six weeks. We are now in about thirty miles of Knoxville, with Burnsides in front of us or at Knoxville, I do not know which. Think there will be a fight in a day or two, unless the Yanks fall back. If we can whip them we can get in the rear of Chattanooga, and Thomas (Rosecran's successor) will be compelled to fall back to middle Tennessee or Kentucky, but it is almost impossible to conjecture what will take place, as a single movement of the enemy may change the entire face of affairs in a day.

I wrote to Mrs. Carter about two weeks ago, and also to Judge Devine, giving him my reasons for not being at the January court. I will write to Brother Charles today. I saw John Kennedy from Camden, South Carolina, this morning. He is colonel of the Second South Carolina Regiment. I used to help him in his Greek and Latin at school. He is one of the handsomest men in the army, and a good officer. James Villipigue is quartermaster. Frank Gilliard is lieutenant-colonel of the same regiment. Henry Green, our old college sheriff, is their chief cook and bottle washer. I was forcibly reminded of my old college days and times, and have had my happiest moments since I left you in meeting old South Carolina friends. They have been my most congenial associates. The air is so chilly and damp that I shall have to cut my letter short, for there is little satisfaction in writing in the open air.

I am getting quite anxious to see you and the children, and occasionally I am very homesick, and always tired of the war, as is every man in the army, without exception. Nevertheless it may prove a blessing in making us all appreciate home and its blessings. I am satisfied there are few or no occasions which are sufficient causes for war; its horrors will never be dreamed of except by soldiers actually engaged in it. Don't be uneasy about the children; make them obey your rules, but do not make your rules severe or numerous. Do not have too many rules on any subject, but have one universal rule—you must be obeyed. Then be cautious how and what you order. I often look from my blanket to the stars and think of the children's' favorite, "Twinkle, twinkle, little star," and wonder if Stark has taught it to Mary yet. I want to see them grow up and love each other, and we can look at them and be happier. I feel like I will see you all again after awhile, and even if I do not there is much consolation in the 11th verse of the 59th chapter of Jeremiah. I have time to read a good deal now when we are camped, and have read several interesting books lately; among them is, "Great Expectations." Oh, how many passages I have read and wished you could enjoy them with me, and we will enjoy them yet.

Give my love to all who love me, and tell the servants to obey you or look out for my ghost. All the Waco boys are well. Billy Dunklin received letters from Frank and the doctor yesterday.

Your husband, faithfully ever,

JOHN C. WEST

LETTER No. XXIV.

IN YANKEE QUARTERS, NEAR LENOIR STATION, NOV. 21, 1863

MY PRECIOUS WIFE:

I am comfortably seated in some Yankee general's or colonel's quarters, by a stove, with a chair to sit in, and a table to write on. It is raining quite hard today, and has been since yesterday. It is just such a raw, damp and uncomfortable day as would have kept me at home if I were at Waco.

I have spent my time thinking of you and the little darlings, and wondering if you can possibly think of me as often as you are the subject of my thoughts. If you do your little school must suffer from neglect or absence of mind.

We, that is Longstreet's corps, left Chattanooga on the 5th of November, and have passed through Cleveland, Athens, Charleston, Sweetwater, Philadelphia, Louden, etc., and are now at Lenoir Station, on the East Tennessee and Georgia Railroad, which runs from Dalton to Knoxville. We have passed through a rich and thickly settled country, which has made me wonder, as I did in Virginia, why any person ever left it to go to Texas or anywhere else. Most of the people whom I have seen were farmers, who were unable to leave home on the approach of the army, having nowhere to go. I saw Major Pearre yesterday. I came on him very unexpectedly seated by the roadside among his wagons and mules, and looking as fresh and as well as ever, and quite natural. He is brigade commissary, and I suppose he has his hands full, as the office is no sinecure. He informed me of the death of old father Harrison, of which I had not heard before. Longstreet pressed on to this place so rapidly that the Yanks had no time to destroy their stores. We captured sixty wagons besides large quantities of ammunition and medical stores. They had fixed themselves in winter quarters, and had built 500 or 600 cabins, nicer and more neatly arranged than most of the cabins on the prairies in Texas, reminding me very much of a well fixed plantation. They are all laid off into streets, with the regularity and precision of a city, with fireplaces, mantel pieces, bunks and stools, and the scoundrels have taken nearly all the sash out of the windows in the neighborhood, as well as cooking and parlor stoves, omitting nothing which would contribute to their comfort or convenience. Our quartermaster took possession of one of the largest and most comfortable.

The greatest curiosity which I have seen is a medical wagon, which is as complete as a drug store, having drawers, compartments and every conceivable size and shape of bottles, with little springs for each vial to rest upon to prevent concussion. There was also a regular cooking stove with utensils in the back part of the wagon; indeed everything which a sick man or a surgeon could want was there. I found a considerable quantity of coffee thrown out on the ground, and have picked up enough to last me some days. I drank a pint this morning, and wished you were here to share it with me. It excites me almost as much as whiskey. Billy Dunklin has found an India rubber ball and given it to me to take home to Stark. The road is strewn with shells and ammunition from here to Knoxville, and there are signs of burning everywhere. Longstreet has Knoxville surrounded and I trust we will capture the entire force. Colonel Tom Harrison is about Knoxville, but I have not seen him yet.

November 22nd: I have no opportunity of sending this to the rear, where it might reach a regular post office, so will keep it until an opportunity offers. Today I have taken a long walk into the country round about, and find that the Yanks have taken everything from the citizens in this neighborhood, chickens, ducks, turkeys, hogs, etc. I succeeded in getting two or three canteens of buttermilk, and gave the old lady three or four pounds of wool which I had taken from the hides of slaughtered sheep. I skinned one sheep and am sleeping on the hide.

November 25th: I have foraged a little today and got two or three canteens of molasses, which my mess enjoyed very much. The people seem to have been pretty well fixed up here. I never saw more beautiful women anywhere; nearly all of them very fair, with black eyes, black hair and pretty teeth. There are many handsome residences, but in a ruined condition, the owners being refugees to the south. I slept last night in somebody's stable lot, under a large oak tree, with the moon straight over my head, and thought that perhaps you and the children might be looking at it and thinking of me. I find it was a good thing to keep my letter, as there is a member of the Fifth Texas who will start for home tomorrow, and will take letters for $1.00 apiece. Yesterday was a very bad and ugly day, but Burwell Aycock and myself concluded to try foraging among the Unionists about here, whom the Yanks have left unharmed, and they, consequently, have plenty of everything. We found very few willing to sell for Confederate money, but by walking six miles we got two chickens, two dozen apples and four canteens of molasses for which we paid $11.00, just one months wages. It rained very hard as we were going back, but getting wet and sleeping wet does not seem to make much difference. My blankets were quite wet last night, but I am all right this morning. I have on no flannels, and just half a foot on my last pair of socks, but will replace them today with a new pair, which one of those fine looking, kind-hearted women gave me yesterday. After Burwell and I got back to camp we could not help joking over the idea of walking six miles through rain and mud for a gallon or two of molasses and a chicken. It is pretty rough, and sometimes serious, but there is something ludicrous in it. We seem not to have Knoxville entirely surrounded. The Yanks have an outlet into Blount county, where they are obtaining provisions. I understand that we are to attempt to capture about 18,000 hogs which the Yanks have penned. There is continued skirmishing going on between our pickets. We had two men killed yesterday; N. P. Moore, of our company, one of the best men in the company, and another in Company D. We can see the stars and stripes waving over the Yankee breastworks. It is said that we will have two more divisions here today, and if so we will have a hard fight tomorrow and capture the town. One of the Fifth Texas was killed this morning. There is a report that our brigade will be sent across the Mississippi this winter.

November 26th: Skirmishing still going on in front, and some of our brigade killed. Selman and Mullens had letters from home today.

Your husband, faithfully ever,

JOHN C. WEST

LETTER No. XXV.
CAMP NEAR KNOXVILLE, DEC. 2, 1863

MY PRECIOUS WIFE:

I have just this moment seen Captain Rust, about to start to Arkansas, and he gives me five minutes to write you a note. I am quite well and hearty, and wrote you a long letter a few days ago, but I am afraid the carrier was captured as we are entirely cut off from everybody by Bragg's falling back. I received a letter from Brother Charles dated October 30th. He says you were all well on October 20th. I have received only three letters from you since I left home.

Your husband, faithfully ever,
JOHN C. WEST

LETTER No. XXVI.
CAMP NEAR KNOXVILLE, DECEMBER 19, 1863

MY PRECIOUS WIFE:

I would like to write you a long letter but it is so windy and disagreeable, and the smoke blows so much in my eyes that I will hardly be able to get through a short note to let you know that I am well. I dream many sweet dreams about you and the children. We are having pretty tough times now; only half rations and half of our brigade barefooted. I was without shoes for two weeks, but have a good pair now.

Macon Mullens, Sam Billingsly, Billy Robinson, Joe Ben Majors and some others, whom you do not know, have been barefooted for three or four weeks, but we have pressed a good deal of leather from the tan yards about here, and several of our men have been shod, and I trust all soon will be. Many letters reach us through Mr. Cushing, of Houston. I have nothing to write which

I would enjoy writing out here in the cold. Billy Dunklin has seen Colonel Tom Harrison. He is well and full of fight.

Your husband, faithfully ever,

John C. West

LETTER No. XXVII.
Camp Near Morristown, December 25, 1863

My Precious Wife:

My first word today shall be to you and my little darlings. A merry Christmas to you, and may God grant us a happy reunion and many pleasant hours ere another twelve months passes by. I shall leave you now and see what a Christmas our soldiers are enjoying with their bare feet and ragged clothes.

December 26th: Well, I had a piece of fried chicken for breakfast, but no bread; but in passing through the regiment found Bennett Wood (brother of Aaron) and his mess had made big hominy; besides having obtained some fresh pork and pure coffee (the latter captured from Yanks). I breakfasted with them and discussed the prospects of getting home this winter and having our Christmas after awhile, as the rumor still floats that we will be sent across the Mississippi this winter. From our regiment I went over to Jenkins' brigade to see Jim Whitner, my old college classmate. He had succeeded in getting two eggs,and Henry, who is on the general's staff, had sent him some brandy. We made a "tom-and-jerry," and enjoyed it very much while we talked over old college days and of friends who have passed to their last account. They were busy as we were in building winter quarters, but Jim insisted on my coming over to dine today, which I did, and have just returned. We had a first-rate chicken pie for dinner, backed by genuine cof-

107

fee sent from home. Was not that glorious for a soldier? What better could he have, unless he was at home with a sweet wife and obedient children?

Sunday, December 27th: The axes still ring busily chopping logs and splitting boards for cabins, as it is said we will be here two months yet, if the Yanks do not run us off. Be cheerful, keep your Latin and music and the little school moving on. It may be a blessing to you some dark day. Trust in God and keep your (powder dry) courage up.

Your husband, faithfully ever,
JOHN C. WEST

LETTER No. XXVIII.
MORRISTOWN, JANUARY 9, 1864

MY PRECIOUS WIFE:

I have an opportunity, the first in a long time, of sending a letter to Texas direct. I did send one about a month ago from Knoxville by a wounded soldier, but as he was quite feeble, I fear you did not get it. I have besides written frequently short letters and trusted them to the uncertain mail, which has been lately established across the river from Meridian, Miss. to Shreveport.

I have written to Mrs. Carter, to Sister Mary and Brother Charles, to Judge Devine and to John A. Green and others, hoping that someone of my numerous letters might reach their destination, and that you might learn that I was well and in good health, and thus feel contented and satisfied. I have received but three letters from you since I left home, one while in Pennsylvania and two at Chattanooga. I fear that many which would have been very precious to me, which would have come as rays of sunshine to a storm-beaten traveler, have been lost by the wayside or been perused by strangers, but nevertheless, you must continue to send them, for if I get one in ten, it will only be prized the more.

Other men in the company have received letters, all of which are sent through Mr. Cushing at Houston. Soldiers are under great obligations to him in this matter. His kindness has sent a thrill of joy to many a weary soul and given strength and courage to sinking hearts. I wrote you about Colonel Harrison. He has been in about one hundred and sixty fights and is a noble soldier. He is getting quite gray but is firm and unflinching in our cause and sanguine of final success. The Waco boys are all well, but like all the rest, nearly all barefooted and half clad. Many of our best men have been killed, and we begin to look like a remnant. It is said that the brigade will be sent across the Mississippi to recruit and be rested, but I do not believe it.

If it is for the benefit of the government, I trust it will be done, as no one will rejoice more than I will at the opportunity of getting home for awhile, but I do not think it practical and doubt the policy very much. You must be contented and happy, and strive to forget me when you have other things to think of, and recollect that your uneasiness cannot help me. Attend to your scholars, your Latin, your music and your children, and you will receive your reward whether I ever return to you or not, for you will be independent of charity from either your friends or the government. Keep all the Bible injunctions in reference to appearing "not unto men too fast." I have not heard from Columbia for some time, owing to the irregularity of the mails. The last time I heard they were greatly distressed because they had not heard from me in two weeks, and wondering how you must feel. I told them you were a heroine and prepared for the little incidents of the war. I do not think I will write you any more except by opportunities to send letters directly across the river, as I have very little confidence in the mail, and feel little satisfaction in writing. You know there is a regular mail established across the river. I live in hopes of hearing some precious words from you.

How I have seen soldiers suffer and be strengthened by the thoughts of home. I have seen many noble fellows fall—better men than I and more worthy to live—and learned afterwards that a noble and Christian wife and little ones awaited them at home, and only received the cold list of casualties without a comment, and the simple but awful word, "killed" opposite his name. This has sometimes happened when a furlough had been promised and was then at headquarters awaiting the signature of the general, but the beneficiary was in his shallow grave before the paper returned to his company. Kiss the little ones and tell the servants to give you no trouble, and never look for me until you see me coming.

Your husband, faithfully ever,

JOHN C. WEST

It was intended that this manuscript should be composed solely of a transcribed copy of diary and letters, but just at this point I am disappointed by being unable to find any memorandum either in diary or letter from the 9th of January, 1864, until the 19th of February, 1864. And it must suffice for the present to say in general terms that during January and February, 1864, I remained with the Fourth Texas Regiment in Hood's division, Longstreet's corps, in East Tennessee, and for a part of that time lived on corn issued to us in the ear from the wagons—three or four ears for man per day; that we shelled, parched and ate it and received nothing else. Parched corn, a pipe of good tobacco, clear water, was the menu for several days. There were barefooted men making bloody tracks in the snow. I heard but little murmuring and saw no signs of revolt. Every man who was there in person and who has a good memory will endorse all that I have written, and say that nothing has been exaggerated and some things very tamely stated. At Richmond, on the 19th of February, 1864, the following order was issued:

[COPY.]

ADJUTANT'S & INSPECTOR GENERAL'S OFFICE,
RICHMOND, FEBRUARY 19TH, 1864
SPECIAL ORDERS NO. 42

XVI. The following named privates will be discharged from the service of the Confederate States: John C. West, Company E., Fourth Texas Volunteers.

By command of the Secretary of War.
JOHN WITHERS,
Assistant Adjutant General.

This order reached our regiment at Bull's Gap, in East Tennessee, on February 26th, 1864. On February 27th, 1864, I received from the Captain of my company the following statement:

CAMP FOURTH TEXAS REGIMENT,
FEBRUARY 27, 1864

KNOW ALL WHOM IT MAY CONCERN:

That this certificate is freely given to Mr. John C. West, Confederate States District Attorney, Western District of Texas, as a testimonial of my appreciation of his services as a soldier while a member of my company, and to his character as a gentleman and a true patriot.

Mr. West entered the military service while constitutionally exempt and holding a position of comfort and ease, which would have shielded him permanently from conscription, and this, too, at a time when the dangers of battle and hardships to be endured had become comparatively familiar to our people, thus showing that he faced calmly and deliberately terrors upon which others had rushed through enthusiasm and excitement. He has conducted himself as a true and faithful soldier on every occasion, having never shirked a duty or missed a roll call from his company.

In taking his discharge from the army, he is but acting upon the earnest and matured counsel of friends who believe that his services will be more valuable to his family and country in the capacity of a civil officer than as a soldier in the ranks.

It is proper to add that this certificate is given without solicitation and at my own suggestion, being moved by the consideration that Mr. West has acted in a manner singularly uncommon and unselfish, and deserving special notice from those who admire true patriotism and self-sacrificing devotion to our country's cause. And while I am glad to see him return to his family and friends in Texas, where he can administer to their comfort and necessities, I deeply regret the loss of his company in camp-life and his example as a soldier.

T. J. SELMAN,
Captain Commanding Company E.,
Fourth Texas Regiment.

I fully concur in the above account of Mr. West, and with pleasure annex my signature.

ED. TILLY,
Second Lieutenant Company E.,
Fourth Texas Regiment.

It will be remembered in this connection that Captain Joe Billingsly and First Lieutenant Allen Killingsworth of Company E., had been killed at Chickamauga on September 19th and 20th, 1863. I was about six feet from Lieutenant Killingsworth when he fell.

February 28th, 1864, Monday: Left Bull's Gap in East Tennessee in company with Fred Makeig, on my way to Texas; walked six miles to Midway Station, which I reached about 11 o'clock. Sat down to await the arrival of the train. Dave Crawford of Columbia, S. C. passed; had a chat with him. Remained at Midway until three o'clock, and took the cars for Greenville; reached there about sunset; called on Captain Lawrence to see about my canteen, which had been borrowed. He had gone to South Carolina.

About dark I went to an old deserted house with the weatherboarding torn off, and slept on the floor. Next morning, February 29th, I walked over to the Thirteenth Mississippi to see Eddleman about my canteen. He had gone to Mississippi on a furlough of forty days, so I suppose my canteen has "gone up for during."

Looked about Greenville all the morning—wet and sloppy—full of Union people; the devoted disciples of Brownlow and Andy Johnson. I met "Ario" Niles here. He belongs to Kershaw's brigade, and was looking for whiskey. I found a very nice looking woman with a pretty baby sitting in the rain, waiting the movements of the cars. I offered her my blanket, but just then the cars started, and she asked my protection to Bristol. I took my seat with her in the ladies' car, and found her a very pleasant and entertaining person—much above the average of a number of others in East Tennessee. I found her name to be Mrs. Mooney, a daughter of Mr. Luttrell, near Bristol. Her husband was in Camp Chase, Ohio. She concluded very properly not to go on to Bristol, as the cars did not reach there until after night, and her father had no notice of her coming; so she stopped with

113

some relatives on the road, and caused them to give me a very nice lunch. I reached Bristol about an hour after night in the pouring rain; could find no accommodations, not even a room to make a fire in. Found a room for the ladies in the depot, and was permitted to stroll up and down under the shed while the rain poured and the wind blew. Remained here until twelve o'clock, when the cars started for Lynchburg. On the train I met Charley Dunlap, Captain Goggin, Dr. Mason and Mr. Harris of Selma, and Mr. Miles; a canteen of whiskey to offset rain and cold and a pleasant time to Lynchburg, which I reached on the evening of the first of March and went immediately to the residence of Col. Augustine Leftwich. Cousin Elizabeth and all the rest received me as kindly and affectionately as possible.

I spent the 2nd and 3rd with them; saw Mrs. Turner and cousin Eliza and Mary Rosanna Clater. The latter is now Mrs. Steptoe; also saw Kate and Minnie Murrell, nieces of Mr. Emerson, an old friend of my mother. They treated me with great kindness and made me feel that I was with real friends. I left Lynchburg on the evening of the 3rd of March and reached Columbia on the morning of the 6th. I found Miss Sallie May Ford with Decca Stark. I went to church with mother and heard a blind paralytic preach a good sermon, and in the afternoon went out to Stark's Hill to see aunties; had a pleasant visit, and went to church with mother at night and heard Mr. Baker preach on the "Gospel a savor of life unto life or death unto death;" witnessed the ordinance of baptism performed in the baptistry in front of the pulpit.

Monday, March 7th: Went to the depot with Miss Sallie May Ford, but there being no train to leave, we returned home, went out to Stark's Hill in the afternoon and stayed to tea. Met Captain Eastman and Mr. Kilpatrick.

Tuesday, 8th: Went to the depot again and found Mr.

Hunt and Dr. Reynolds; had quite a pleasant trip to Kingsville, where we remained for three hours. Saw some Yankee prisoners pass on their way to Georgia. Saw a nice
looking girl and had some conversation with her; we
started for Camden about 4 o'clock. At Statesburg met
Bishop Davis and his daughter, Miss Lila, Miss Cornelia
Elmore and Miss Martin. When my name was called the
pretty girl whom I had met at Kingsville rushed up to me
and proved to be my cousin Abby Gamewell. Reached
Camden about 6:30 and had a busy time attending to
the baggage of five ladies; put Miss Cornelia and Miss
Martin in General Cantey's carriage and rode with them
to John Gamewell's, where I am now. Met at the depot
also Misses Ella and Essie Reynolds.

Wednesday, March the 9th: Went to the cemetery first
after breakfast. Abby Gamewell accompanied me; found
the old city of the dead much enlarged and improved.
Our enclosure is in very good condition but has a more
neglected look than is proper for my mother's grave. Oh,
why did she leave me so soon and why should we be so
widely separated now? Is this to be eternal? God forbid
that eternity should fail to disclose the wisdom and jus-
tice of her removal. Thus far time has not revealed the
reason for this act of the Almighty. The hidden mystery
is yet unexplained, whereby the destiny of a soul has
been changed for all time. Shall it be for eternity? Oh,
God, in whom I trust, make known thy ways to me.

Passed through Camden; saw many changes not worth
noting; saw Sam Shiver, Mr. Cureton, Mr. Cook, John
McCaa, Dan De Saussure, Jim Villepigue, John Kennedy,
Godfrey Peques, Mr. Hughston, Mr. Dunlap, Billy McKa-
in, William E. John son, Bob Johnson and Judge Withers.
Discussed the constitutionality of the conscript and substitute law; referred to Halliburton of Georgia and Vance
of North Carolina. Called on cousin Abby Capers; Mary

115

Wragg was in school and Sallie at the factory. Came to cousin Catharine Lee's and found no one at home. After dinner called on Colonel Chestnut and family; saw Miss Hattie Grant. Colonel Chestnut is almost gone and Mrs. Chestnut very low. Mrs. Reynolds and Miss Ellen came in about dark. Our old servant, Harriet, called to see me; is looking old, and told me that her daughter, Lizzie, was to be married. I gave her $10.00. I came back to Mr. Gamewell's about dark; found cousin Isaac and Elizabeth Alexander there, looking not much changed.

Thursday, the 10th: Called at Bishop Davis'; all well and quite natural. Miss Lila is looking as young as ever. Went to see the Dunlaps; found the house and grounds much improved, and family as genial and kind as in the olden time. Miss Ann is now Mrs. Leitner, and has a nice little girl, Sallie Cook, plump and healthy.

Charley's wife quite pretty; was a Miss Cunningham. Muggy is fifteen and quite handsome. Ann Kennedy grown out of all knowledge. I forgot to say that I called on Cousin Catharine Lee this morning; she looks much broken and very sallow. Came home to dinner, tired and weary. John McCaa had just left, having called to take me out to dinner. In the afternoon Mary Wragg, Sallie and Sophia Zemp called to see me. They have intellectual faces and fine eyes. Sophia is like her father and yet a Reynolds. I saw Mrs. William Gerald also. At dusk went with Abbie to Cousin Catharine Lee's and took tea. Charley Bonny came in and kindly offered his horse to me during my stay. Went home about 9 o'clock. Am now about to write in album and think I shall try the following: "As all the Christian virtues, without charity, are as sounning brass and a tinkling cymbal, so without modesty are all the traits which distinguish the truly noble woman. It is the center around which all the virtues and all the faculties must revolve. It is the glass through which all that is beautiful and good must be viewed, as the cord to the kite, the rudder to the ship, the curb to the bit, the cornerstone to the edifice, the keystone to the arch, thus is modesty to the temple of the soul; without it all is weakness and confusion."

Friday, March 11th: Rode Charley Bonny's horse to Kirkwood. Called at Mrs. Holmes' to see Sallie Ford; also on Mrs. W. E. Johnson, and took a look at the old pond. Went to see Miss Cornelia Elmore at Mr. Shannon's. Found Miss Mattie Shannon quite agreeable, but apparently sad. I took dinner at Mrs. Dunlap's; had an old time dinner, and a pleasant visit generally. After dinner I called on my old teacher, Mr. McCandless; he was not at home, but I had a long chat with Mrs. McCandless, in which she told me of her troubles and excited my sympathy. I took tea with Cousin Abathia Capers and her children. Came home at 9 o'clock.

March 12th: On coming downstairs found that Mr. Gamewell had come home yesterday evening. He is getting quite bald and gray. We walked out in the garden and orchard and examined the fruit trees, of which he has a great number and many varieties. Not feeling very well I returned to the house, while Mr. Gamewell spent the day pruning and trimming. In the afternoon Mary and Sallie Capers and Sophia Zemp came up; went to take tea with McCandless, but found him out; spent a pleasant evening enjoying music by the children, etc.

Sunday, March 13th: In the morning heard the Rev. Wightman preach at the Methodist church; text, "Let him take up his cross daily and follow me." Attended the Episcopal church in the afternoon. Sat with Alfred Brevard. After church walked home with McCandless. Took a drink and stayed to tea.

Monday, 14th: At 2:30 o'clock a.m. Miss Cornelia Elmore called for me. We went to the depot; met there

Miss Sallie May Ford and Mrs. Chapman, a sister of Mr. James Connor, of Charleston. Had a pleasant trip to Columbia; have remained there since, enjoying it hugely.

Monday, 21st: Left Columbia at 4 o'clock in charge of Mrs. Waties, who has proved a most charming companion. Made traveling acquaintances as follows: Lieutenant Todd, of Lexington, Kentucky, a nephew of Mrs. Abraham Lincoln; Colonel Hunter; Major Duxbury, of Hood's Staff; Mrs. Middleton, wife of Captain Middleton, who was wounded at Dandridge, in Gracie's Brigade. No unusual features about the trip until Tuesday morning, when it snowed quite a storm, but made the scenery along the road most magnificent. The bowing pines and evergreens were rendered picturesque and beautiful. Near West Point we had quite an interesting episode, there being a smash-up on the track among the freight trains. We were compelled to get out and flounder through the mud, around the wreck, and take a box car to West Point, which we left on the afternoon of the 22nd, and with no particular incidents reached Montgomery about 2 o'clock a. m. Went to Montgomery Hall and found things quite cheerless and uninviting. Got a poor breakfast and am now awaiting the arrival of the boat in order to go on to Selma. Mrs. Waties has proved a perfect blessing on the trip and time has passed on light and noiseless wings.

Thursday, 24th: Left Montgomery on the *Southern Republic* for Selma. The boat is magnificent. The trip was as agreeable as the times afford. Reached Selma at 10 o'clock Friday morning, 25th, and was detained all day until 7 o'clock on Saturday. Slept with Murford Smith. Left Selma Saturday morning for Denopolis, which I reached at 10:30 on same day.

Saturday, 26th: Went to General Polk's headquarters. Found Tom Jack very kind. Told me to call next day to see what could be done. I rode out to Waties' battery and messed with Lieutenant Waties. Took tea at Dr. Reese's nearby.

Sunday, 27th: Read Jean Vol Jean and took dinner with Dr. Reese.

Monday, 28th: Got soaking wet on the way to the depot and stood out in the river about two hours, and finally got the boat headed down stream by main force, and reached McDowell's in time for the train, which took me in five miles of Meridian to Old Marion. Paid a negro $5.00 to carry my carpet bag to New Marion. Remained there all night, paying $5.00 for a poor supper and a good bed.

Tuesday, 29th: Left New Marion at daylight on a construction train, and reached Meridian, or rather the spot on which it formerly stood, in about an hour. Found nothing but desolation, ashes and ruin. I went to see the quartermaster, but he was absent. Spent most of the day trying to devise some means of getting to Enterprise, but failed. About 10 o'clock in the day met Amos, mail carrier for Ector's brigade, and a soldier called Dock, from Polk's army, of Tarrant county, Texas, on their way to Texas. They concluded to go to Enterprise, and start out from there with me, so we contented ourselves with the prospect of remaining at Meridian until the next evening to await the passenger train from _____.

Wednesday, 30th: Found Ellick McKaskill, formerly of Camden, South Carolina, an engineer, and learned from him that his engine would go to Enterprise in half an hour. I got aboard and reached Enterprise at 9 o'clock. Went immediately to the quartermaster's office to see Major Theobald, to whom Colonel Tom Jack had written a note in my behalf. The major was absent, but Mr. Frazell, clerk, was very kind in assisting me to find a saddle, for which I paid $30.00. Major Theobald soon came in, and after some discussion let me have a small black Indian pony, gentle, and in good condition. This discussion was had out behind the tent, and I was assisted by a bottle of French Brandy, out of my carpet sack, and which had been thoughtfully placed there by mother (Mrs. Stark) in Columbia, South Carolina.

Amos, Dock and myself, soon packed the pony and started from Enterprise about 2 o'clock. Crossed the Chickasaw at the junction of Oketibby and Chucky, and went about ten miles by dark, walking and leading the packed pony. We stopped at the residence of Sam Howze, who was very sick. Just after supper there was a great shrieking of females and calls for help. Supposing the bed, or one of the children to be on fire, I rushed into the room and found Mr. Howze speechless in a spasm. I assisted in rubbing him and soothing the children, who were screaming at a terrible rate. He soon got better and all was quiet again. We returned to rest, and slept well on the floor of the piazza. We left immediately after breakfast.

Thursday, 31st: We went over a flat pine country, very muddy and disagreeable for about five miles, then through a rolling sandy pine and black jack country to Paulding, passing through this place. We stopped for lunch about one o'clock about one and a half miles from it, where I am now writing, and where I will probably remain for some time, being overtaken by a great catastrophe. Our pony, which we foolishly trusted too far having eaten his fill, has kicked up his heels and left us in the road, high and dry, forty miles from everywhere and no hope of getting anywhere. Dock and myself have tried for an hour to track him, but have failed. Amos and Dock are now on the same business, and I alone in my glory am minding the baggage until they return. I am afraid their search will be fruitless, but I trust in

Providence and hope for the best. This brings my diary up to fifteen minutes of four o'clock on the afternoon of March 31st, 1864. At half-past five Amos and Dock have returned, having trailed the pony two and a half miles into the Claiborne road, and then lost the trail. We are in a sad condition and a heavy storm of rain coming on. We have concluded to go back to Paulding and try to get a horse, and spend tomorrow hunting for the pony.

April 1st, Friday: All-fools' day, and proverbially unfortunate for all undertakings. I procured a mule from Dr. Walton, and having learned from Mr. Bradley that the pony had been impressed from Mr. Sanders sixteen miles on the Claiborne road, I started in quest of Mr. Sanders and the pony. I heard of the pony all along the road and felt quite elated thinking the four hours' ride would set me all right, but fortune has frowned thus far, for I have been to Sanders' house and the pony is not there. He gives me good reason for believing that he is in the neighborhood. I have been to Dr. Dillard's, Mr. Jones', Mr. Gavin's and Dr. Wheeler's, where I now am. Dr. Dillard advises me to remain here until dark and perhaps the pony may turn up. I am very nervous and very hungry, and will remain until morning, and then return to Paulding, and then—and then—what? I do not know. I am lost and cannot imagine what course to pursue, but I think I shall turn back towards the army. I doubt whether it would be right for me to attempt to walk one hundred and sixty miles through a thinly settled country, with no companion and no acquaintances on the road, and without knowing at what point to cross the Mississippi.

May God preserve Mary and the little darlings and enable me to meet them at some time. I have stated my case and my troubles to old Mrs. Wheeler. It does not seem to strike her that I may be hungry, but I am. Hurrah, the pony has just come up to the lot according to Dr. Dillard's prediction.

Saturday, April 2nd: Started from Dr. Wheeler's yesterday evening at 6 o'clock, found the pony too stubborn to be led, dragged him about two miles, then paid a negro five dollars to ride him to town; got there at eleven o'clock p.m.; found a note from Dock and Amos saying they would meet me four miles from Paulding at ten o'clock in the morning, so this morning I was up bright and early and at the four mile post by nine o'clock, but no Amos nor Dock, nor could I hear of them on the road. I went on for two miles, saw some Indians on their way to the playground, but too much worried to notice their peculiar "tricks and fixings." Met Lieutenant Carter, who advised me to take the Raleigh road, which I did. Found an empty wagon and put my carpet sack in it for ten miles and rode the pony. Stopped at and got dinner from Dr. Simelle and then went four miles further to Duncan McLaurin's. Talked about Sherman Case, etc. My horse was well fed and I was well taken care of and my bill five dollars.

Sunday, April 3rd: Left McLaurin's at 8 o'clock and have made good time. Stopped at Raleigh to get Colonel Lowry to endorse General Pope and the Secretary of War. Got dinner for two dollars from a camp of negroes; best I have had since I left Columbia, except at Dr. Reese's. I am now at Captain Ward's, four miles from Raleigh. Lost my saddle blanket today.

Monday, April 4th: I left Captain Ward's at half past seven. He charged me nothing; I appreciate this. I traveled a lonely, very lonely route through the pine land as barren as the sea-beach; passed occasionally some beautiful creek bottoms tilled with magnolias and jasmines and stopped at half-past twelve and took a cup of coffee, went on and stopped at Mr. Churchly(?) where I am now. A very nice gentleman and lady have just come up in a buggy. I am sorry for them. I learned that Camp Fitzhugh left them four days ago. I have never seen or heard of him since we went into the battle of Gettysburg. I supposed he was captured or killed.

Tuesday, April 5th: The gentleman and lady who arrived last night were Mr. McCormick, sheriff of Jefferson county and Mrs. Kennedy, a Creole widow of New Orleans, very handsome and quite attractive. She is on her way to Crystal Springs and availed herself of McCormick's escort as far as Hazelhurst, thirty-five miles beyond this place. This morning Mr. McCormick very kindly relieved me of my carpet sack so that I have ridden today and made over thirty miles through the same lonely, desolate country, made more supportable by the company of Mrs. Kennedy. Stopped at Mr. Welch's, three miles from Hazelhurst.

Wednesday, April 6th: Started early and got to Hazelhurst in time to take a seat with Mr. McCormick in his buggy; tied the pony behind and got along finely for three or four miles, when pony broke the rope; got down and tied him again, when he again pulled back, broke the rope and started on the back-track; by good fortune a stage driver stopped him before had gone a quarter of a mile. I mounted and rode him to Mr. Gorden's, eighteen miles from Hazelhurst, where I now am; will go on to McCormick's, which is thirty miles, tomorrow, and hope to cross the river on the next day.

Thursday, April 7th: Left Mr. Gordon's about 9 o'clock; got on very pleasantly until about 11 o'clock, when a heavy rain set in. I got soaking wet and remained so until I reached McCormick's, where I was treated with great kindness, furnished with dry clothes, etc., and remained until morning.

Friday, April 8th: Left McCormick's at 9 o'clock and

rode to Oakland College, and went to Major Jannary's; found a party just starting for the river, and so had to travel on until dark through almost impassable ravines and swamps; reached the river safely, and much to my surprise found Joe Cobb, John Sparks and Frank Smith and quite a crowd of soldiers waiting to cross, also an old gentleman with quite an amount of tobacco. We perambulated the river bank all night until daylight, watching the arrival and departure of the skiff, which could only carry two men at a trip, having two horses to swim each time. My turn came after daylight, but I got over safely with the pony; could see Yankee gunboats above and below me on the river.

Saturday, 9th: I am six miles west of the river, having had a good breakfast, the first food I have eaten for twenty-four hours, and having pony fed the first time since yesterday morning. Thank God for His goodness to me thus far, and may He soon grant me a happy meeting with my precious wife and little ones at home. I stopped at Mr. Major's about 4 o'clock, sixteen miles from St. Joseph's.

Sunday, April 10th: Left Mr. Major's at 8 o'clock and traveled through a terrible miry road for twelve or fourteen miles, swimming one bayou. We stopped at a house on Bayou Mason for dinner, then moved one mile beyond Winsboro.

Monday, April 11th: I rode on and crossed Boeff river at Columbia, and went on to Ouachita crossing at Columbia and came seven miles this side, making thirty-six miles; stopped at Widow _____, a dirty, filthy place.

Tuesday, April 12th: Made a long ride today, passing Vernon and stopping at Mr. Sims', five miles west of Vernon, a neat and comfortable place, well managed and quiet.

Wednesday, April 13th: Rode forty-two miles to Burnett's, six miles east of Mindon—a good stopping place.

Thursday, April 14th: Rode to Shreveport today and met a good many of Wharton's men on their way to Texas, and saw my brother, Charles.

Friday, April 15th: Left Shreveport about 9 o'clock; rode thirty-five miles and stopped at Mr. Granbury's, ten miles from Marshall.

Saturday, April 16th: Reached Marshall about 10 o'clock a.m; saw Mr. Bacon and Mrs. Bayliss and Mr. Vanderhust; rode on to Mr. Fisher's, thirty-five miles from Tyler; passed some Yankee prisoners on the road.

Sunday, April 17th: Rode from Mr. Fisher's to fourteen miles beyond Tyler, making about fifty miles; could not stop until half-past 10 at night, owing to the unwillingness or inability to entertain on the part of the people on the road; a barren, sandy country.

Monday, April 18th: Here ends my diary, which leaves me about 100 miles from Waco, my home. I have no written record of the remainder of the trip, but remember distinctly that the pony, only about thirteen hands high, was put to his mettle and reached Waco late in the evening of April 20th, 1864. I kept him as a souvenir until after the war closed, and had many a glorious and delightful day with him in the woods, where deer and wild turkeys were abundant. He became a family pet, and with hounds, horn and gun, his memory is interwoven with some of the happiest associations of my life. He bore the classical and euphonious name of "Button," as I learned from Mr. Sanders in Mississippi.

Here now follows my discharge based on the order from Secretary of War heretofore given:

SOLDIER'S DISCHARGE

To All Whom It May Concern:

Know ye that John C. West, a private of Captain T. J. Selman's Company, Fourth Regiment of Texas Infantry, who was enlisted the 9th day of April, one thousand, eight hundred and sixty-three, to serve for the war, is hereby honorably discharged from the army of the Confederate States. By order of the Secretary of War. Said John C. West was born in Camden, in the State of South Carolina; is twenty-nine years of age; five feet, eight inches high; fair complexion, blue eyes, light hair; occupation when enlisted, a Confederate States District Attorney for Texas. Given at headquarters, Fourth Texas Regiment, this 19th day of February, 1864.

T. J. SELMAN,
Captain Commanding Company E.,
Fourth Texas Regiment.

Approved.

J. P. BANE,
Lieutenant-Colonel Commanding.

Here is a copy of the original order for transportation given me by Hon. Thos. M. Jack:

HEADQUARTERS, DEMOPOLIS, ALABAMA
MARCH 26, 1864.
To MAJOR J. C. DENIS, T. M. GENERAL.

MAJOR:
The Lieutenant-General Commanding desires you to issue transportation to Mr. John C. West, District Attorney, to cross the Mississippi River.

Respectfully, Major,
THOS. M. JACK, A. A. GENERAL

This order is endorsed as follows:

HEADQUARTERS, DEPT. LORING'S DIVISION,
APRIL 3RD, 1864.
Guards and pickets will pass J. C. West unmolested.
By order, ROBT. LOWRY,
Colonel Commanding.

126

I have referred to Lieutenant Todd, a nephew of Mrs. Lincoln. He was very kind and courteous in giving me directions and making suggestions as to getting across the Mississippi, and wrote in my notebook and signed his name to the following memorandum, which I keep as a souvenir of those eventful days:

From Shubata to Monticello; to Brookhaven; to Fayette via Union Church. Arriving at Fayette, ask for Mr. Duncan in town, and Colonel Harrison one mile out on the Waterproof road. Oscar Wood lives half way between Fayette and Waterproof. He will send you to B.A. Service, living opposite Waterproof. He will cross you. Go to John Tellis, eight miles from the river on the Independence road. He will send you across Tensas river, too.

R. S. TODD.

And so ends for the present, the "plain, unvarnished tale" of "A TEXAN IN SEARCH OF A FIGHT."

ADDENDA

THE STORY OF A BLANKET

When I left Waco, April, 1863, to join the army of Northern Virginia, I had with me a large shawl and a very large blanket. This blanket was made of pure wool, grown, spun and woven in McLennan county, the handiwork of Mrs. Powell, who lived near Bosqueville. It was striped after the fashion of Mexican blankets, which were quite common in Texas at that time. The colors were green, red and yellow, so intermixed and interwoven in stripes as to be quite unusual and noticeable. My prudent and ever watchful wife took the precaution to write my name, company and regiment on a piece of white tape in indelible ink, and sew it securely in a corner of the blanket.

At Kingsville, South Carolina, this blanket and shawl were under the seat upon which I sat April __, 1863, but when the train reached Columbia they were both gone. I have never seen the shawl since that day. I regarded them as lost to me and my heirs forever. I remained in Columbia a day or two and was supplied with a blanket and other articles by my sweet mother-in-law, Mrs. Theodore Stark, whose blessed memory will be a joy to as long as I live.

I went to my company on the Rapidan, then to Culpepper, and through the Gettysburg campaign.

Marched up and down the beautiful and picturesque defiles of the lovely Shenandoah with its bright and shining waters until the mountain trails from Snigger Gap to Ashby Gap became familiar roads, and wading the river two or three times a day was a pastime, but in September, 1863; four months after my blanket disappeared, we went with General Longstreet to Chickamaugua's bloody field, and after gaining that Pyrrhic victory we moved to the foot of Lookout Mountain and held a long line up and down Lookout Creek for two or three weeks in October.

While in camp here I learned that my old college friend, General Mart Gary, was within a mile of our brigade. I got permission to visit him and found him at his headquarters on a gently sloping hillside. There had been a very hard rain the night before and hundreds of blankets and other articles were spread and stretched out to dry. While we chatted I viewed the interesting scene, one of the most unique and striking in army life. About 200 yards away I spied my Texas blanket and said to Gary, "Yonder is a blanket I lost in South Carolina several months ago." Gary was disposed to be profane and replied, "The hell you say." I called his attention to the blanket spread out in the sunlight on some bushes with its gaudy colors glistening in the sun. He said, "Well, let's go down there and see about it." We went and I showed him the piece of tape in the corner with my name on it. By being wet the wool had shrunk and made a sort of roll on the edge of the blanket so that this mark could not be readily seen. Gary looked around and said in a loud tone, "Where is the man who claims this blanket?" Someone replied, "He's out yonder at work on the redan." Gary said, "Well, tell him here is a man from Texas who claims this blanket." We walked away to headquarters with the blanket, and then some man said—just like a soldier will—in a distinct but somewhat suppressed tone, "Where is the man that stole the Texas man's blanket?" and then someone else—just as a soldier will—in a little louder and more distinct tone said, "Where is the man that stole the Texas man's blanket?" And then two, three, 100, 500, took up the refrain with higher inflection until the woods resounded in every key with, "Where is the man that stole the Texas man's blanket?" and the echoes from the foot of Lookout Mountain answered, "Blanket!!!" I had not seen Gary since my graduation in 1854. We talked of reminiscences of college days—of present hopes and fears—for an hour or more and parted never to meet again. I returned to my camp, and on the next day was visited by Mr. Horton, of Lancaster, South Carolina. I think he was a sergeant. He said, "I am the man who had 'the Texas man's blanket,' and I have come to tell you how I got it." He was very pleasant in his manner, and we talked for sometime. The substance of his story was that his wife had received the blanket from a soldier in Lancaster District; that the soldier was sick and stayed a day or two at the house, and gave her this blanket as he had more than he needed. (I suppose he had the shawl also). That his wife had sent him the blanket from home, and he had it only a few days before I found it. We parted very pleasantly. His statement seemed very reasonable and I was satisfied he stated the real facts. This was about the 20th of October, and this wandering blanket served its purpose well during the severe winter campaign in East Tennessee, protecting me from many a wintry blast, warding off snow, sleet and rain. I brought it back to Texas in May, 1864, and kept it for many years. In 1868 I took it on a camp hunt on Manos' Creek, about fifteen miles from Waco, and while we were absent from camp, in the drive, the blanket disappeared, and I have never seen it since. Some months afterwards a citizen informed me that he was sure that Mr. _____, shady character, carried the blanket to the Indian Territory, where, doubtless, it now envelopes the dusky form of some heroic Minnehaha.

SPEECH
DELIVERED AT McGREGOR, TEXAS, BY JUDGE JOHN C. WEST IN 1897, ON DECORATION DAY.

Comrades of McGregor Camp and Fellow-Citizens:

Every assembly of the people ought to have for its chief object the benefit and profit, not only of those who call the meeting, but also of all who witness its proceedings or take interest in its objects and purposes. We have met today not only for social intercourse with each other and pleasant communion for the sake of "auld lang syne," but to publish to the world and discuss the purposes of this organization, to increase its membership and thereby increase its power for good. In addition to the benevolent and sympathetic work at home among its own members, to assisting the distressed and needy and burying the dead, one of its chief aims and objects is to act as an auxiliary to the general union of Confederate Veterans, to assist in perpetuating the glorious and untarnished record of Southern soldiery and the true history of a cause the memory of which is dear to every Southern heart, and ought to be interesting and instructive to every lover of truth under the shining sun, for it involves the origin and growth of the doctrine of individual liberty and local self-government, the bed-rock foundation of true civil liberty and human happiness, the chief objects for which men live. Our surroundings today recall the bitter memories of thirty years ago, its marches, its struggles, its triumphs, its failures, its victories, its defeats; its tears, its joys, its blood and sufferings, its final disaster, its apparently hopeless ruin. How

133

memory draws aside the curtain and dwells upon the pictures of the days gone by! How aged men and women love to turn and look back through the vista of the paint upon the chances and changes of other times; and even the hardest trials, and scenes filled with tears and blood and broken hearts and shattered hopes, are dwelt upon with a melancholy pleasure.

Philosophy and religion and time, the great healers of many woes, and work and labor—those all-conquering balms—have left no place for fruitless weeping and unavailing regrets, and yet we hear men say, "The winds of other days blow on my forehead."

> *Poor old voice of eighty, crying after*
> *Voices that have fled;*
> *All I loved are vanished voices,*
> *All my steps are on the dead.*

In those sad and doleful hours of 1865 the men and women of the South, houseless and homeless, with ashes and desolation on every side, with lowering clouds in the sky and no sure safety on the earth, seemed with the energy of despair to have put past behind them saying, "Let the dead past bury its dead," and looking with hopeful eyes to the future in imitation of faithful soldiers upon the field of battle, they faced to the front and cried, "Forward," and forward they have gone from that dark hour to this.

And here the thought is suggested that we have two audiences before us: the old and the young; those under forty years of age know little of the times of which we speak except by tradition.

When we address ourselves to the discussion of religion or politics or financial and economic problems the audiences is as one man—an equal interest is exhibited and felt by all alike. The discussion of the "almighty dollar"will command earnest thought and attention while a history of the trials of the past will fall upon dull and listless ears. But a people who have no regard for their own history and whose children have no pride of ancestry will soon become degraded before the world and make proper subjects for the ambitious schemes of designing demagogues. It is well for these younger men and women to hear part of the history of days gone by, to listen to the mother as she tells of the departure of husband, sons and brothers to the "cruel war," of restless days and sleepless nights, and weeks of bitter waiting for news from the field, for "the letter that never came," when neither telegraphs nor railroads were known in Texas, and months sometimes pass while hearts were sad and eyes often dim with tears, and anxiety and "hope deferred" would turn brown locks to grey. It is well for the boys to hear fathers recite the tale of marches, sieges, battles they have fought, and to see the old soldier fired with the memories of other days, shoulder his crutch and show how fields were won.

Most, if not all, the leading and most conspicuous characters of the South who were noted for statesmanship and fiery eloquence before the war and for courage and military genius during that trying period have passed from the stage of action, but "their deeds, their worthy deeds, alone have rendered them immortal." The study of their lives is the study of the history of the South and of the war. The biography of Lee, of Davis, of the Johnstons, of Beauregard, of Kirby Smith, of Jackson, of Hood and a hundred others are epitomes of history of our country and there can be no better use of time and no higher inspiration to noble character than for the young men and women of our day to read, to study and reflect on the lives of these men and their kindred spirits who have built for themselves their posterity "monuments

135

more lasting than brass," more enduring than marble; and to this end I would suggest that each Camp in Texas should have a fund for the purchase of cheap editions of histories and biographies, that a librarian whose residence should be central be selected to be keeper of these books as the property of the Camp to be loaned out and used for a reasonable time under proper restrictions by the members of the Camp and their families. In this way a dozen volumes or more could be used in every neighborhood, knowledge would be free and easily accessible, thought would be aroused, discussions had, books would be searched and compared. Occasionally a good reader, young or old, might be chosen to read aloud in the presence of the Camp and families, some interesting selection from history or biography. Zeal and curiosity would be stimulated and instead of gossip and tattle and nonsense there would be profitable conversation, there would be a wiser and more thoughtful generation.

This suggestion is merely thrown out as a hint that may be utilized and if it bears good fruit our meeting will not be in vain.

What was the cause of the war between the states? Was it to abolish slavery or to settle the question of the right of secession, or were both involved? So far as history shows, there seems to have been no definite terms of settlement as to the right of secession. The reconstruction acts seem to be based on the theory that the seceding states were out of the Union, and were to be received back again on conditions and limitations, but a disavowal of the right to secede was not among the conditions, and there is no amendment to the Constitution of the United States which refers to or hints at such a condition. The question, so far as the abstract right is concerned, is still open and unsettled, and if Massachusetts were to secede today, there is no agreement or act of settlement to which she could be referred as conclusive of her right in the premises. (See note. * *)

But time and reflection and experience, as well as the sword, have demonstrated that the practical application of the right to secede is but the entering wedge to final dissolution of the Union and subversive of the chief object of the Federal compact, to-wit: to regulate commerce, and to present an undivided front as one people to the nations of the world.

With the results of the war and the experience of thirty years, we have facts and elements and experience before us not conceived or dreamed of by the fiery and sentimental statesmen and patriots of former days, and we are divested once and forever of the real bone of contention, to-wit: slavery, which, whatever may be said to the contrary, was the "apple of discord" without which it is difficult if not impossible on any reasonable hypothesis to account for an overt act on either side; and while the preservation of the Union was the declared purpose of the invasion of the South and was the basis of a "war cry" which appealed effectually to patriots, south as well as north, yet the inner and germinal question of slavery was the real cancer which poisoned the entire blood and circulation of the body politic, and for years threatened final dissolution and was in fact the only subject of that "irrepressible conflict" which was beyond reason or agreement simply because with the South it resolved itself into the elemental question of the right to hold against the world property, the right of possession and ownership of which, had been legalized and had descended from father to son for more than two hundred years.

But more than two generations in the North and many persons in the South had given much thought and study to the subject, and large majorities in the North, and many individuals in the South, had greatly changed or modified their views on the question, and with many thousands it had become a matter of conscience. In England and other countries the discussion had received a fresh and growing vigor, so that the world had become a unit in condemnation of an institution, the existence of which was regarded as vital and essential to the existence of the South, so that the abolition of slavery, and the abolition of the prestige and power of the South were to the Southern soldier one and the same, while the destruction of the institution and the preservation of the Union were to the Northern soldier likewise one and the same—for with slavery there could be no permanent and friendly Union.

Following the discussions and various compromises which had been contemplated for many years previously, Hon. John J. Crittenden (U.S. Senator from Kentucky for more than twenty years) in the session of Congress, of 1860 and 1861, proposed an amendment to the Constitution of the United States, by which slavery, except where it already existed, should be recognized and confined exclusively to the territory South of latitude 86.80, being about the center of the State of Missouri. The proposition failed, and is only mentioned to show that among the last things discussed before separation and bloodshed was the issue of slavery. We will not pursue the matter further as these thoughts are merely thrown out to excite the interest of young men and induce them to study philosophically the history of the past, and thereby be better prepared to meet the issue of the future, and if these crude thoughts lead to closer study and to wise conclusions the purpose of their delivery will be accomplished.

In all properly conducted public gatherings there is an inspiration for the young, the flags, the badges, the mottoes, the music, the march—each and everyone stirs the heart and stimulates the mind to inquire, "Why all this concourse? What moves the hearts of fathers and mothers so? To the young mind all that passes before it becomes an object lesson. Well do I remember that more than fifty years ago in the historic town of Camden, South Carolina, as I trudged along the way to school my eyes rested every day upon a simple marble shaft supported by a granite base, and upon the shaft were written these words:

"HERE LIE THE REMAINS OF
BARON DE KALB,
A GERMAN BY BIRTH, BUT
IN PRINCIPLE A
CITIZEN OF THE WORLD."

And Oh! how that phrase "in principle a citizen of the world," has echoed and re-echoed in my heart a thousand times. It filled my mind with questions, and in answering them I learned that De Kalb, though born under a foreign flag, came to America with Lafayette—that other grand and noble hero—to offer his sword and his life in behalf of freedom's cause; that he was with Washington at Valley Forge; that in the battle of Camden, August, 1778, he fell at the head of Delaware and New Jersey troops, pierced by eleven wounds, in a desperate charge upon British guns, and thus his blood bedewed the sacred soil of South Carolina and illustrated in his death that the real hero is "in principle a citizen of the world," and bares his breast in the cause of local self-government wherever the cry of the oppressed is heard, and asks not whether numbers and resources are in his favor, and at each returning Spring, after more than a hundred years have passed, amid waving palmettoes and sighing pines, the children of South Carolina bedeck the tomb of the gallant foreigner who declared

139

by his death that in principle he was a citizen of the world, and so did brave Pat Cleburne leave the shores of grand old Erin's isle, and so did he yield his life for truth and liberty on Franklin's bloody field. To his proud spirit peace, and eternal glory to his name. And so must questioning spirits today learn that we are here to recall the honorable deeds of faithful and devoted men who were willing to test on the field of battle their fealty and devotion to the doctrine of local self-government—the keystone of the arch upon which true republicanism and democracy must rest. It was to try the extremest phase of this doctrine as applied to the states of the American Union that the war between the states North and South was inaugurated and fought to a bitter and baleful end. Did the right to secede belong to the states? was the general issue. Did any state have a right under its powers of local self-government to adopt and enforce a law by which one human being could be held as a slave for life by another? was the special issue which overshadowed the first in the eyes of the world, and placed upon the South a burden never borne by any other people, and put us single-handed and alone in a contest against the nations of the earth; but the teachings of our ancestors of the North for more than two hundred years and the practice and theory of the government for nearly a hundred years prior to the sad disaster had taught us no distinction between one kind of property and another, and so, with no other purpose or instinct than the universal one of the right of preservation of life and property, we entered into the most remarkable and bloody contest of modern times, the right and wrong of which must be settled in another age and by impartial history. We discuss it not today.

And so it was the men who wore the grey came face to face with those who wore the blue, and in this Southern land how life was changed. There "were hurryings to and fro" and sudden partings such as press the life from young hearts, and sighs that ne'er might be repeated. The husband left his wife and never again did she see his manly form. His face is but a memory, and though years have passed his image greets her yet, and sadly she sits and sings, "Thy bright smile haunts me still." And, Oh! that mother's parting with her only son. She thought her heart would break and broken, indeed, it is, for he fell on Manassas, bloody plain, and there he lies "unknelled, uncoffined and unknown," and as the winter of age gilds her hoary head, she reads in the "book of books," "The Lord is nigh unto them who are of a broken heart," and sadly she bears the whispered promise—some sweet day—on some sweet day "we'll meet again."

During those four dark years nearly every man in the South under sixty years of age, and every youth, over sixteen, was in some form or other engaged in the contest. Only think of it! Every man engaged in war, and, that too, at times which seemed to be one of extermination; every woman knitting, sewing and stitching day and night without a murmur, frowning upon every coward and urging by smile and threats every man to the front—becoming themselves the sinews and nerves of the contest. Oh! patient, diligent, brave women of the South—worthy mothers of as brave and noble sons as ever bore a banner or unsheathed a sword. Well might the poet say:

> *The world was sad, the garden was a wild,*
> *And man, the hermit, sighed till woman smiled.*

Not Egypt with Semiramis and Cleopatra, nor the old dispensation, with Rachel and Rebecca, and Hanna, nor the new with Martha and Mary and Dorcas, nor Greece with the mothers of Epaminondas and Alcibiades, nor Rome with her Cornelias; nor France with her Joan of

Arc and the splendid women of her salons, nor England with her line of queens, nor Scotland with her highland heroines, nor all the world can boast of feminine worth more excellent and exalted than the genuine true heroic Southern woman, the highest and noblest type of "God's best gift to man." And what kind of men did these women send to the front? Let us not boast of ourselves. The testimony on this point shall be the truthful and candid admission of one whose statement will not be questioned by any man North or South. I refer to that generous, true and high-toned soldier, General U. S. Grant. In his correspondence with General Butler, from City Point, August 18, 1864, he says:

> I am satisfied that the object of your interview had the proper sanction and therefore meets with my entire approval. On the subject of exchange, however, I differ with General Hitchcock. It is hard on our men held in Southern prisons not to exchange them, but it is humanity for those left in the ranks to fight our battles. Every man we hold, when released, becomes an active soldier against us either directly or indirectly. If we commence a system of exchange which liberates all prisoners taken we will have to fight on until the whole South is exterminated. If we hold those caught they amount to no more than dead men. At this particular time to release all rebel prisoners North would ensure Sherman's defeat and would compromise our safety here.

Such testimony from such a source stamps the Southern soldier as the true type of an unconquerable people. What more can be said? What use have we for rhetoric and figures of speech, when we have the candid judgment of the greatest soldier among our foes—one of the

142

most wonderful men produced by that wonderful strug-
gle—saying substantially: These people under the ordi-
nary rules of war, involving exchange of prisoners, on
equal terms, can never be conquered, except by extermination. What higher tribute can a soldier pay to his
opposing foe than to say: I have met an army in which
every soldier seems to have said, "Give me liberty or
give me death," and I see no means of victory but extermination. It is to embalm in the hearts of coming generations the precious memory of the valor of such men as
these that we meet today to tell the story of their woes,
to weave these garlands and scatter flowers upon their
last resting place. It is fit that these girls and maidens
fair should hear the story of the true and brave, for one
of the highest incentives of the true Soldier to deeds of
daring is the memory of the smiles of "the girl he left
behind him," and many a time, and oft around the camp
fire, have we heard him say:

> *None but the brave, none but the brave!*
> *None but the brave deserve the fair.*

Then drawing from beneath his ragged jacket an image
which had given him strength and inspiration on many
a dreadful day, I see him smile and hear him say, in the
language of bonnie Scotland's sweetest bard:

> *Auld·nature swears—the lovely dears*
> *Her noblest work she classes, O*
> *Her prentice hand she tried on man*
> *And then she made the lasses, O.*

Friends and Comrades! behold the banner which they
bore (turning to the Confederate flag). From Gettysburg
to Glorietta thy folds have kissed the breeze; on a hundred well fought fields the victory has been thine; many
a time we have seen the friend who bore thee fall, another and still another bear thee on triumphantly; we have

heard his frantic appeal, "Men, come to the flag," and have followed with flame and smoke and sabre stroke and death-shots falling thick and fast like lightning from the mountain cloud, till hope seemed gone forever. We have prayed to the God of battles to sustain thee, but by his decree thou art fallen and furled forever, and yet we love thee:

Tho we were doomed to wonder on
Beyond the seas, beyond the sun,
Till our last weary sands were run
Till then and then we'd love thee.

Sleep in thine own historic night—
And be thy blazoned scroll
A warrior's banner taking its flight,
To greet a warrior's soul.

The reference heretofore to Mr. Crittenden leads to a reflection on a peculiar phase of the civil war which these young people can scarcely realize; I mean its character as a war between friends and brothers of the same blood.

Hon. John J. Crittenden was for twenty-four years a United States Senator from Kentucky. He was twice attorney-general of the United States and also governor of Kentucky.

The political situation must have been much discussed and thoroughly understood in his family and household, and yet see how honest men under the same surroundings and teachings may differ and fight over a question of right or conscience. His son, George B. Crittenden, was a major-general in the Confederate States army; another son, Thos. L Crittenden was a major-general in the army of the United States. Here are two other cases: Captain Percival Drayton, commander of United States steamship *Pocahontas*, was a brother of Thos. H. Drayton, commanding Confederate troops in South Carolina. Major Lea, on the staff of the Confederate General Magruder, was the father of Lieutenant Lea, of the United States Navy, and in the capture of the *Harriet Lane* at the Battle of Galveston the father and son came face to face, Lieutenant Lea being mortally wounded, but survived long enough to receive the kind attention and benedictions of his father whose breast was a pillow for the head of his dying son. Thus the heart's blood of the boy in blue stained the bosom of the father in grey. Methinks I hear the father say:

> *But let me see; is this our foemen's face?*
> *Ah! no, no, no, it is mine only son,*
> *Ah! boy, if any life be left in thee*
> *Throw up thine eye; see, see what showers arise*
> *Blown with the windy tempest of my heart*
> *Upon thy wounds that kill mine eye and heart.*
> *O! pity, God, this miserable age*
> *What stratagems, how fell, how butcherly,*
> *Erroneous, mutinous and unnatural*
> *This deadly quarrel daily doth beget.*
> *O! boy thy father gave thee life to soon*
> *And hath bereft thee of thy life too late;*
> *These arms of mine shall be thy winding sheet;*
> *My heart, sweet boy, shall be thy sepulcher,*
> *My sighing breast shall be thy funeral bell.*

The body of the boy in blue was tenderly laid to rest in southern soil by southern hands and the sod is bedecked with blooming oleanders in each returning Spring and the sad waves of the sea sing an unending dirge o'er fratricidal war.

Numerous other instances could be given of brother in arms against brother, of father against son, brother-in-law against brother-in-law, and sometimes as in the case just cited, meeting face to face in deadly conflict. With these sad and terrible details before us it ill becomes us to bandy such epithets as fanatic! traitor! rebel! There was neither treachery nor rebellion, but there was on both sides a firm and unwavering devotion to principles which each held as dear as life and for which each shed his blood as a libation to the cause of truth and maintenance of that highest principle of civil liberty, the greatest good to the greatest number, each resting his judgment upon the training and the conscientious convictions and teachings of his ancestors for a hundred years prior to the contest.

Let the mantle of charity cover the mistakes of the past. We are all back at the old homestead under the roof of our fathers. Let us dwell together in unity.

In behalf of peace and happiness of posterity let prejudice cease and reason rule. While our children learn that the fallen banner, now furled and furled forever, was bathed in the blood of as brave soldiers as ever faced a foe; let them also be taught that the questions at issue were settled never to be renewed or re-opened, and that the Stars and Stripes, the emblems of our common country, is the flag of the South as well as the North; the flag of the Union baptised in the blood and fires of 1776 and re-consecrated and confirmed in 1861-65, by the flowing wounds of the worthy children of revolutionary sires. It is the same banner under which our fathers, led by the immortal Jackson, fought at New Orleans in 1815. Under it New Mexico and California were added to the Union and some, doubtless, present here today who saw it wave in triumph over the halls of the Montezumas. It is the ensign of an empire grander than Caesar's legions gave to Rome, and of a government whose constitution is a shield of its own people and the admiration and model for kings and princes of the world. (Turning to the American flag):

146

Flag of the brave! they folds shall fly
The sign of hope and triumph high!
When speak the signal trumpet tone
And the long line comes gleaming on.
Ere yet the life-blood, warm and wet,
Has dimmed the glistening bayonet
Each soldier's eye shall brightly turn
To where they sky-born glories burn
And as his springing steps advance,
Catch war and vengeance from the glance.
And when the cannon mouthings loud
Heave in the wild wreathes the battle shroud
And gory sabres rise and fall,
Like shoots of flame on midnight's pall,
Then shall thy meteor glances glow—
And cowering foes shall sink beneath
Each gallant arm that strikes below
That lovely messenger of death.
Flag of the free heart's hope and home
By angel bands to valor given,
Thy stars have lit the welkin dome
And all thy hues were born in heaven!

NOTE.—Since the speech was delivered, I have found the following extract in a newspaper referring to Virginia:

In good faith, she re-wrote her constitution, inserting in her Bill of Rights the following clauses:

Article I, Section 2. That this state shall ever remain a member of the United States of America, and that the people thereof are a part of the American nation, and that all attempts, from whatever source or upon whatever pretext, to dissolve said union or to sever said nation are unauthorized, and ought to be resisted with the whole power of the State.

Section 3. That the Constitution of the United States, and the laws of Congress passed in pursuance thereof, constitute the supreme law of the land, to which paramount allegiance and obedience are due from every citizen, anything in the Constitution, ordinances or laws of any State to the contrary notwithstanding.

That is now the organic law of Virginia, the law by which every citizen of Virginia is bound, and how, with that declaration before him, any citizen of Virginia can claim that this state has the right to withdraw from the Union is to our mind inconceivable.

MRS. MARY ELIZA WEST
Born in South Carolina, May 11th, 1836
Died at Waco, Texas, April 11th, 1903

PASSED TO THE HIGHER LIFE

MRS. MARY ELIZA WEST, OF WACO—
HER GOOD WORKS AND THE END.
By A. R. McCollum in The Waco Tribune,
April 18, 1903.

MRS. MARY ELIZA WEST, wife of Hon. John C. West, of Waco, is dead. She breathed her last on Saturday, April 11, about six o'clock in the evening, on Easter Eve. This community, the people who knew and loved her, has joined in rendering the last rites of love and esteem, in laying her mortal form to rest in beautiful Oakwood cemetery, a spot she loved and had for years aided to make lovely and restful. It is the simple truth when we say the whole community has had part in this last, tender office of love. Mrs. West has been in impaired health for months. Early in the year there was ground for hope that she would enjoy health and strength and usefulness again. With her to be useful was part and parcel of life; she enjoyed it as much as she did health. But a few weeks ago recurring pain and weakness warned her family that the fond hopes of the new year were not to be realized. The end was not long delayed. A brief mention in these columns last week warned readers of the impending culmination. It came as above stated, on a day replete with sacred suggestions and trust, the eve of Easter.

BIOGRAPHICAL AND REMINISCENT.

Born in Edgefield, South Carolina, on May 11, 1836, Mrs. West was of honorable Colonial ancestry. She was the daughter of Major Theodore Stark and Eliza Carey Lamar, his wife, both families of the old regime, coming from Huguenot lineage, with traditions and memories that run back to the Edict of Nantes. Her childhood and

150

earlier girlhood were spent in Edgefield and Columbia. In the latter city she was educated and graduated in the old Muller's Academy, of high repute in antebellum days and was known there as an exceptionally bright girl, with a high order of intellectuality, giving promise then of the rich attainments of later years. In 1858 she united in marriage to John C. West, a young lawyer of her state. It was an auspicious union of young people congenial and by social station fitted each for the other. It was to be a long and happy wedded life for it lasted virtually forty-five years. Tuesday, April 14, would have been the forty-fifth anniversary of the union. The body lay all day in the open casket, that was imbedded in flowers. Death had effaced every line of age, and left the calm, lovely face beautiful. It was that of a young matron once more. Surely Death must have in it much that is beneficent for all of mankind, for its seal on the face is that of peace and rest.

LAST RITES.

IMPRESSIVE SCENES AND SERVICES AT THE CHURCH AND CEMETERY. Easter Sunday, April 12, at 5 o'clock in the afternoon, was the hour fixed for the burial of Mrs. West, the religious services at the First Baptist church, where she had membership. By the hour named the attendance exceeded the seating capacity of the room and many stood on the outside, on the grass plot or went away. Promptly at the hour the casket was borne down the central aisle by the following active pall-bearers: John T. Battle, W. H. Jenkins, J. D. Shaw, C. L. Johnson, T. J. Searcy, and Walter Gregg. Honorary pall-bearers: Chas. B. Pearre, John F. Marshall, Ed Rotan, W. T. White, F. L. Carroll, J. Hansel Wood, John Moore, and S. P. Brooks. The casket was literally covered with flowers. The Mary West Chapter, D. of C., Daughters of the Revolution and delegations from other organizations mentioned above had seats assigned them and took their places. Mrs. B. R. Davis, of the Daughters of the Confederacy, added to the impressiveness of the occasion. She took her stand near the casket and held in her hand a Confederate flag. She held the staff so the silken emblem drooped over and rested upon the casket.

Near the casket sat the husband, children and other relatives of the dead. Profound silence prevailed for a few moments and then music was heard. It was the splendid choir of the First Baptist church, chanting that grand and tender anthem, "Nearer My God to Thee."

Rev. B. H. Carroll, for twenty-five years the pastor of the First Baptist church (in which Mrs. West had held membership over forty years) then arose and opened the service by reading the following passages from the Scriptures:

> And when Jesus cried with a loud voice he said Father, into thy hands I commend my spirit; and having said thus he gave up the ghost."—Epistle of St. Luke, chapter xxiii, verse 46.

> But he (Stephen) being full of the Holy Ghost looked up steadfastly into the heaven and saw the glory of God and Jesus standing on the right hand of God.

> And said, "Behold I see the heavens opened and the Son of Man standing on the right hand of God."

> And they stoned Stephen, calling upon God and saying, "Lord Jesus, receive my spirit."

> And he kneeled down and cried with a loud voice, Lord, lay not this sin to their charge. And when he said this he fell asleep."—Acts of the Apostles, chapter vii, verses 55, 58, 59 and 60.

And I, John, saw the holy city, New Jerusalem, coming down from God out of heaven, prepared as a bride adorned for her husband.

And I heard a great voice of heaven, saying, behold, the tabernacle of God is with men, and he will dwell with them, and they shall be his people, and God himself shall be with them and be their God. And God shall wipe away all tears from their eyes, and there shall be no more death, neither sorrow nor crying, neither shall there be any more pain; for the former things are passed away.—Revelations, Chapter xxi, verses 2, 3 and 4.

Dr. Carroll's remarks were brief, occupying but a few minutes of time; but he spoke with deliberation and manifest emotion, explaining how long and intimately he had known Mrs. West—for thirty-five years, and twenty-five of those years as her pastor. He gave a biographical sketch (the leading facts embodied in another part of this article) dwelling on her life as a Christian, a wife, mother and member of society, passing to the closing days, when she was awaiting death. He had visited her during those hours and had talked and prayed with her. The appropriateness of the scriptural passages read by him at the opening was illustrated, happily and forcefully by an episode he related. She had lain silent with closed eyes for hours—when all at once those around her saw the eyes open and look upward and forward. Reaching out her hands she exclaimed: "Daylight, all is daylight! Jesus is holding my hands! I see and understand now as I never did before!" And in her eyes there was ecstasy, joy and trust that cannot be described in words. And then the preacher told of her last loving words of farewell to the husband with whom she had walked so long, "and I doubt not," said Dr. Carroll, "that she saw the new Jerusalem, the angelic hosts, and that God received her spirit, as he did that of the martyred Stephen; that Jesus, who had held her hands, while she went through the valley of death, welcomed her to the Holy City, beside the River of Life." Dr. Carroll closed his remarks with the statement that at the desire of the family the final words of the service would be by Rev. John G. Kendall, as a cherished and intimate friend of the deceased.

Mr. Kendall, the widely known Baptist minister of this city, now stepped near the casket. He, too, spoke briefly as to the time consumed. Indeed, the simplicity, the absence of all ostentation, in the last rites the people of Waco could pay to this woman so beloved of all, was notable. It was an expressive tribute of the entire community, yet wonderfully impressive and touching because of the absence of anything that savored of mere pageantry or ceremonial. Mr. Kendall seemed to feel all this, and that the heart of the sorrowing people was speaking through his lips, for in earnest, tender words, each word so well chosen and eloquent that it was as a cameo of expression, he told of his acquaintance and experience with her while she was in life. "In my visits to the home where sorrow and pain was to be found," he said, "I have found this beloved woman more frequently than any other. Where there was need or destitution, in the dwellings of the poor and lowly, she visited and ministered. Where there was sickness, suffering or tribulation, where death had come and comfort and aid was in order I have found her. Not once, twice or thrice or occasionally, but often and steadily. And this was not alone within the bounds of our denomination. It was general and where sympathy and help was needed for she knew no creed or limitations." He spoke of her practical interest in all movements or undertakings for moral upliftment; of her kindly and wholesome influence in the upbuilding of the community, of her gracious force in social life, her exalted womanly character. The value of such work and example, he said, was incalculable, and computation could hardly be made of its influence. It was rich in example and encouragement, rich in the testimony it bore to the verity of God's love and mercy, pledged and secured to man through Jesus the Christ.

Rarely, if ever, we feel warranted in saying, have Drs. Carroll and Kendall spoken more feelingly, more forcefully, more instructively, on occasions of like character. Each, as said above, spoke briefly, in simple terms, yet each paid an eloquent tribute and drew the lesson of Christian faith, of a Christian life. Dr. Kendall, when he closed, asked that the gathering be bowed with him in prayer and his invocation was a fitting finale to his remarks.

Then the choir sang another hymn. It was "Rock of Ages," and was rendered with so much impressiveness that as the sound of the voices and organ died away a deep hush fell over the vast audience and for an instant the quiet was absolute. The pall-bearers now moved out of the room, bearing the casket to the street, and the several societies and organizations mentioned before followed, taking the places assigned them in the funeral cortège, which moved slowly down Fourth then to Fifth street and out to Oakwood cemetery. For a mile or more this funeral procession extended—hundreds of vehicles in the line, while the trolley cars running to the cemetery were crowded also. These reached Oakwood first and a vast gathering had formed around the West family plot of ground before the slow moving cortège arrived. It was eminently fitting that Mrs. West should be laid to rest in Oakwood. For years the cemetery has been one of the many local institutions that received her thought and loving effort. She had aided materially in the care, maintenance and beautifying of this spot and knew every foot of ground in its limits. That it is as beautiful, as worthy of local pride as it is, is as much due to her as any one. She knew she would sleep there some day and where she would lie, and in that place they put her grave—beside that of a baby grandson who was the first of the name to rest there. Her open grave, as the vast assemblage formed around it was seen to be literally walled with flowers. So thick were the flowers that no trace of earth could be seen. The closing rites were of the simplest nature. While the casket was lowered into the grave the choir sang, "Asleep in Jesus." And as the grave was filled, "Shall We Gather at the River?" was sung, changing finally to "Yes, We Shall Gather at the River." Rev. Dr. Carroll then came forward and pronounced the benediction. It was grandly simple, the last scene was as the dead would have had it. By request of the family all semblance of ostentatious ceremonial was avoided and only old, well known hymns were sung. The mound under which Mrs. West's body rests was one massive heap of flowers—they covered it from head to foot. And with a last look at this mound those who mourned and sorrowed, the family, friends and vast concourse went away. It was truly a representative gathering—all classes of society, so many religious faiths were there. Rich and poor, old and young attended and it should be mentioned that among these were many negroes, some of them old ex-slaves, who had known and loved the dead lady, who had known her kindness and blessed her for her bounty—her goodness to them. Their sorrow was manifest.

We could write at length of the goodness, the graciousness, the beautiful life, the usefulness of this beloved woman, whose two score years and more spent here were worth so much to this people. But that is not needed, for the memory is here enduring. Not one of those who knew her will ever forget. Nor shall we speak of the loss those nearest and dearest to her have sustained. They know it only too well and so do we all, who sorrow and sympathize with them. They have some priceless memories—memories of the long years of companionship with the wife and mother, her love and devotion. They have her example, her fragrant life as an inspiration—and this community has that too. Few men have had the privilege as the husband has had, of nearly half a century of wedded life with a devoted wife. Few children have the loving care of a mother as long as hers had. Death entered into their family circle so rarely. Husband and all her children live. It was their sacred privilege to be by her side and minister with loving hearts and hands during her last hours. It was their privilege to commune with her in those days, to witness scenes that were hardly of earth. The episodes of that week are too sacred to dwell on them, but one we shall venture to relate. It was so full of beauty, of inspiration, of strength. On Wednesday prior to the end, Rev. B. H. Carroll and wife called during the morning. He had been her pastor for many years. She said: "Tell him to sit on the bed beside me, take my hand and pray." He did so, and offered a touching and simple prayer. An hour after his departure the dying woman (for she was then in the darkness of the Shadow of the Valley) suddenly opened her eyes wide. They were aglow with ecstasy. Her face beamed with the radiance of heaven. In a voice clear and strong, such as the watchers had not heard during her illness, she exclaimed: "Daylight! daylight!" and looking around and upward she added: "All is daylight." A moment later, stretching her hands upward she added, "Jesus hath both my hands." These were the last words, but those who were there will never forget the scene-the ecstasy in her eyes, the radiance in her face, and the joy and exultation in her voice. So impressed were the watchers that with once accord they were moved to sing in a low tone a verse of "Nearer My God to Thee." It had been given to them to witness a transfiguration. The long life as a Christian woman could have left no doubt as to her faith in the verity of God's promises, but even had there been such doubt every vestige would have vanished with this experience. She had been told she would not dread death when it came, would not taste its bitterness, and she did not. All was peace, all was trust, all was "daylight." It is easy to believe that on the beautiful Easter day here, when the church bells rang out "Resurrexit! Christ has risen!" when loved ones and friends gathered for a last earthly look at the still placid face, beautiful in repose, the freed and enraptured soul had realized, was experiencing its immortal boon and destiny—that it found its home in the city not made with hands, that it abided in peace and content in the light that comes from the presence of the Father, where all is "daylight." Who would barter or lose that hope and trust? God have mercy on us, weak mortals that we are, and strengthen us—give us to live as she lived and at the end know the glory and the love and the mercy of the infinite as she did. Amen.

www.ingramcontent.com/pod-product-compliance
Lightning Source LLC
Chambersburg PA
CBHW020337100426
42812CB00029B/3154/J